# Feeling lost and Finding My Way

## ABOUT THE AUTHOR

Motivated by his personal experiences and passion for practical education, Andy delivers workshops and inspirational training events for business leaders, young people and creative entrepreneurs. He has a gift for connecting with people, inspiring positive change and making things happen – and that's what he does.

After escaping a hard fought time with depression and struggling with anxiety, he's now an ambassador for mental health awareness and emotional wellbeing.

Andy is from Newcastle and lives in London.

Visit www.andydunn.co or email hello@andydunn.co to get in touch with Andy.

Feeling Lost and Finding My Way.
Andy Dunn

2nd Edition, Originally Published Dec 2016.

ISBN: 0995686718
ISBN-13: 978-0-9956867-1-7

Brand Design and Artwork by
Juliana Vignette and Rory Lawrence

# Feeling lost and Finding My Way

**Andy Dunn**

# BOOK REVIEWS

"Your honesty and bravery will open people's hearts."-*Jakub. G.*

"Truly amazing. It will speak to so many people. Your story is yours, but the lessons are for all of us to learn. The journey is intriguing and vivid, I didn't want to stop reading. It's like an exciting novel, and I couldn't wait find out what happened…"-*Charlotte. P*

"A good balance of sentiment and humour."- *Michael. F.*

"Motivating and inspiring. Your story truly had me wanting more. I was able to put myself in your shoes, which helped me reflect on my own past, present and future life choices."
-*Jovanna. C*

"It gave me a different perspective on mental health"- *Helen. K*

"Powerful and positive. Your journey filled me with hope for the future. A great insight for people who have loved ones suffering too." – *Becky. L*

"Andy's story tells us mental health can effect everyone and we can get through difficult times. He keeps us part of his story all the way through. Very helpful and thoughtful, the honesty makes it accessible"-*Jason. M*

"Wonderful and so inspiring" – *Claire. A*

"Friends…they cherish one another's hope.
They are kind to one another's dreams."

- Henry David Thoreau

# thank you

To everyone who has helped me on my journey to make this book possible, I thank you all so much.

Especially to Mum and Dad, Kate, Terence, Wayne and Louise, Lisa and Jasmine, and all of my early readers. In your own way, you've given me the love, support and belief to make this happen.

I share my story with courage and an open heart. I trust it will reach the right people at the right time.

Much love,

*Andy*

# CONTENTS

"People take different roads seeking
fulfilment and happiness.
Just because they're not on your
road doesn't mean they've gotten lost".

- Jackson Brown Jr

# FOREWORD

Everyone reading this now will have their own reasons for picking up or downloading this book and for wanting to read Andy's story. You will all bring your own experiences; you will all take your own thoughts away. There may be struggles and insights that you share, or recognise in others close to you; you may come to an acceptance of your own journey, where you are now or the path that you need to follow in your own time.

For each of us we have a different journey to make, with unpredictable stops and turns. Sometimes we step confidently, sometimes we need to wait a while, or find a new path. Reading Andy's open and courageous story of his own hopes, struggles and self-discovery was at times a difficult and emotional read, because of our instinct to protect those that we love the most. It is a reminder of the important role that we have as parents, teachers, educators, family and friends to guide and offer support, but also to know when to step back and give time and space for dreams and aspirations to be moulded and take shape.

Knowing how to be there, and knowing how to share the darkest places is perhaps the hardest of all; knowing when to listen, knowing when to say nothing, and being comfortable with the uncomfortable.

But Andy's story is also one of hope, of finding strength through adversity, and of finding fulfillment and self-acceptance.

Andy's Mum

1

# Welcome to the Journey

# INTRODUCTION

My life was great, until anxiety overwhelmed me. I was happy and I had a promising future, until depression brought me to my knees. I didn't really think about what was next, until I had too.

It hit me after University, the first moment I decided to consciously direct things and take control, to think ahead and answer the looming questions of "what are you going to do?" "What do you really want?" "What is holding you back?"

The pressure felt defining and the honest search was exposing.

In the back of my mind, there was a pressure for the next step to be the right one, as if I was searching for a reason to make it all make sense, to make the last twenty-two years of my life worthwhile and to start the next chapter in a direction that felt true to me.

In a huge world of opportunities and possibilities, I wanted to know where I belonged. I wanted to find a place I could make a difference. I believed there was a purpose I had to find. I was battling with the expectations of others, I wanted to make people proud, but deep down I also wanted to find my own way.

Whilst this is my story, parts of it may be yours, or that of someone you know. I share my story not because I think it's unique, but precisely because it isn't.

My name is Andy, I was brought up in Newcastle with loving parents, an amazing family that gave me the upmost love and support. I progressed through school with relative success; I skipped off excitedly to college and University; I worked hard and got a 1st class degree. In the eyes of education, I'd made it.

All was beautiful…until it wasn't.

I suddenly went from being a cheerful chappy, to plummeting into a deep depression with no idea of how to escape. I felt lost, alone and disconnected.

The education system and society can create immense pressure at such a young age. Before we've had a chance to explore the world, before we really know ourselves, before we know what's possible, we make choices and define ourselves. We limit what we think we can do and who we think we are, or who we think we are not. One of the motivations for writing this is to relieve some of the pressure a lot of young people feel, to have it all figured out and know what to do.

This story is about how I learned to listen to my own inner voice, to create a life that I wanted to live. And it's an invitation for you to listen to yours and create the life you want to live too. I know my desire to feel fulfilled and to express who we really are, is certainly not unique.

As you read this book, I'd like you to remember two important things. Firstly, that this is a story written from my experience, written from an authentic and honest viewpoint. It's not academic research or a manual to tell you how you should live your life. I'm not a counsellor or a trained psychotherapist. I share experiences I've had and the journey I've been on, in the hope that you'll be able to relate to it or learn from it. It's up to you how you interpret this book and apply it to your own life. I want to be as truthful as possible, so you can be too.

The second thing is to be open to a journey of your own. If you read it with an open mind, it's likely to provoke questions in yourself. It may help you reflect on your own life, choices you've made and your plans for the future. If it does so, be compassionate with yourself, even if you can't describe exactly what it is. And remember there is support available if and when you feel you need it.

For a lot of people, feeling lost, however you describe what it means to you, often co-insides with mental health struggles. The racing thoughts and complex feelings, the desire to understand what's going on or where you are, there's often a need to make things make sense. The pressure we put ourselves under can make life very difficult to cope with.

## Mental Health Awareness

One of the motivations for writing this book is to be another bold voice in the arena of mental health and wellbeing, encouraging people to have difficult conversations when they need support, to inspire people to talk about their feelings and to let people know, that when they are struggling, others are too. If we all hold our silence, we all think it's just us; we perpetuate the shame around mental health issues and we suffer alone.

Before I went through depression, I thought I was the only one. I didn't know friends or family that had struggled. And I certainly didn't think it was okay to talk about it. I felt so much shame and embarrassment. I didn't want people to feel pity. I didn't want to ruin the image people had of my out-going and happy character. I didn't want to show weakness. I didn't know what to say or how to talk about it.

Through telling my story and exposing the challenges I faced, I hope to encourage others to talk about how they are feeling too. To let people know, that when they are struggling, they are not alone. If we all hold our silence, we all think it's just us; we perpetuate the shame around mental health issues and we suffer in silence.

## Guiding Other People

You may be reading this to understand more about people around you. I once had a very good friend who lost their way and went off-track in life. The feelings and experiences they went through were very reminiscent of my own. At the time I had no idea how badly they were struggling. I tried my best to support them as a friend would do, but in truth, I was very naive to the extent of their possible suffering.

I tried to be inspiring, supportive and get them back to the path I thought they wanted to be on, instead of helping them in a way they needed. I felt awful for not knowing how to help such a good friend and I just didn't really know what to do.

I want people to read this book and be more aware of what people can go through without the outside world knowing. I kept thinking to myself, if all this has been going on for me and very few people know about it, then there is probably a lot going on for other people that I have no idea about either. And it's not that everybody needs to divulge everything they hope for and struggle with, but I do want to inspire more people to have open conversations about emotional wellbeing and mental health.

Despite lots of amazing work around the world, there is still a huge stigma. I am doing my bit to open people up to important conversations.

Whether life is good or not at the moment, whether you are reading this for yourself or to support someone else, I really hope it helps in some way.

It's time, to begin the journey.

# Feeling lost and Finding My Way

Andy Dunn

Chapter 1

# A NEW BEGINNING

"If man does not keep pace with his companions,
perhaps it is because he hears a different drummer.
Let him step to the music he hears,
however measured or far away"

Henry David Thoreau

It was finally over. I could breathe for the first time in months. In March 2011, I had no idea I was about to spiral into a deep state of depression, that my perspective on life would crumble and I'd enter a place I didn't know existed. A place so low and so dark I'd need a lot of help to get out.

Six months before my emotional crash, I was a buoyant graduate with a first class degree. I had a spring in my step, and after four years of hard work, I was ready to take on the world! I wasn't quite sure which direction I'd take next, but I felt qualified to do something worthwhile.

At the intersection of my first major life decision, the fear of being without a plan and without anything to strive towards scared me. I felt alone for the first time in my life and I didn't know how to cope. I felt nobody understood how I was feeling and nobody could answer the questions I had. I was scared and confused within myself and with what job I should work towards doing.

I desperately wanted somewhere for my life to go because I wasn't happy where I was. More importantly, I wasn't happy with who I was. Having a career with a success ladder was much more appealing. An excellent way to distract me from addressing personal challenges I had.

When I was at University, my life was so busy that I didn't have the time or I didn't create the time to think about my future. The insecure part of me gave my already hard work ethic an extra boost to squeeze every minute of work and fun out of my days. In some ways, this kept me more grounded and focused in the moment, but when it inevitably came to an end, it left me lost. It left me exposed.

I was searching for an exciting career to transfer the energy and attention to. One of the reasons I felt so much pressure to choose a mesmerising and exciting career, is because I knew that's where I'd be able to succeed. I thought, if I succeed, I can get all of my life's fulfilment – how wrong I was. If I were successful, it would make it easier to deal with other aspects of my life – time would tell.

Where was I going to get this creative fulfilment I desperately craved?

*

As a young child I revelled in the times I got to play and make things. I was always encouraged to express myself and use my hands to follow instructions from the wandering wonders of my mind. I'd sit on the floor in our living room for hours and hours, surrounded by Lego and building blocks, continuously exploring the unlimited possibilities in front of me. From Lego to K'nex and K'nex to Mecano, I was always eager to see a structure come to life. After school, I'd run home to watch the latest episodes of Art Attack and follow it with making lots of mess, to my parent's mixed approvals, depending on the scale of the mess.

In moments I was alone or trying to relax before sleeping I'd pick up a sketchbook and attentively copy my favourite cartoon characters. After having my mind blown by the wonders of Disney World at a young age, I was captivated by the magic. Every time I put pen to paper, I felt like I was reliving the energy of the theme parks. I'd put all my attention into the intricacy and detail of cartoon drawings. And by the same token, I was able to drift off into a quiet blissful place that gave me the time to just be.

On our family holidays to the beach, we would build huge sand castle cities and dig a deep moat all the way around it, all working together to create something special before the tide would come in to sweep it away. Then we would do it all again the day after.

As I got a little older and computers started to command our attention, I'd build theme parks on Roller Coaster Tycoon, model cities on Age of The Empires and animate cartoons on a Simpson's computer game. I didn't so much mind what I was creating, only that I was creating something.

As I progressed through secondary school, I was determined to keep my creativeness alive and hold onto any outlets that would let me make things. But in a world where academia is king, it's not so easy. For anyone that has good academic ability, it becomes a battle to continue a creative path.

Subjects like Maths, Science and Languages are the chosen ones, they are selected as indicators of our ability to succeed in life. They reflect our intelligence and they reflect how good you are and how good your school is. Creative people are often cast away with a feeling of 'that's not as important'.

I was stuck in the middle. I was academically capable and also highly creative. I knew I shouldn't have to choose. That there is a time and a place for complex algorithms and theories of medical study, and an equally special place for creativeness in all it's forms, for inventors to shape the world; for artists to decorate our life with inspiration and for everything in between.

I was stuck between fulfilling my academic potential to get high grades and exploring an unknown and uncertain journey of creativity. I believed that on some fundamental level creativity was important and it should be treated as though it was. That it shouldn't be a comparison or a trade off with academia.

But I was in the system and had to follow the flow.

Unfortunately, I had to make a choice.

In my A Levels, I tried to keep my options open; I chose Maths, Design and IT. I chose IT because I thought it would be useful to be computer savvy and it didn't have any formal exams. I wasn't particularly good in exam conditions and I didn't actually think they were always a fair measure of applicable intelligence or skill. I chose Maths because I liked to solve problems and I chose Design because it seemed useful and a lot of fun.

But as soon as Maths got overly complex and IT became boring, I diverted almost all of my energy to my creative world once again. I skipped math's lessons to go to design classes and I spent my IT homework time doing additional Design coursework.

I was inevitably choosing to go the creative way. My design teacher really believed in me and I felt that's where my passion was taking me.

Thankfully at the end of my secondary school journey, my design teacher pointed me towards Art College. A place I could fully embrace all my creative gifts and get wonderfully lost in a place full of other creative people.

But even though my enthusiasm was as high as ever, I struggled to get in. I was more technically minded than overtly artistic, so I didn't have many examples of "creative work". A Levels in Math's and IT weren't very impressive to an Art Director. All I had was a small portfolio of Design work and a few average paintings from my GCSE days. And I wasn't good at painting at all, nor did I have any intention of becoming so. I pleaded and pleaded that I was creative enough and I prove it. I didn't know where my career was going; I just knew this was the gateway to a creative degree, and I wanted one of those. Thankfully, I got in.

After a year at Art College, my options were whittled down to Graphics and Advertising or Product Design. I liked the creative side of advertising campaigns, but I was less interested in becoming a graphic designer. The Graphics course was hugely popular and I figured that if it was as competitive in the real world, and I didn't really want it, I definitely wouldn't make it.

Product Design only had a handful of people so I thought it was a better option. I could once again learn to make things, all be it a little more complex than Lego. I would begin to master the art of designing and manufacturing things.

At University, I delved into a world of design that gradually merged with manufacturing. Our tutor was a carpenter extraordinaire and we were surrounded by technical expertise and high-tech machinery that allowed us to build anything we could imagine. Before I knew it I was welding, turning wood, making moulds and forming plastic. I was learning about industrial manufacturing processes, the history of design and how it shapes our everyday life.

It wasn't how I envisioned my life panning out, but I was happy learning, experimenting and making things.

*

As our degree came towards the end, a few of us agreed we'd like to continue making things. There were only eleven people on our course, so we all became incredibly close. Five of us thought about starting a business together. How hard would it be to start a business? We'd supplement our income with part-time jobs - when we got to grips with things properly - that would slowly fade out. We'd be able to design and make things to our heart's content!

In the month after graduating, we faced the daunting step into the real world. Our safe learning environment was gone and we had to decide what to do next - to get a job, start a business or continue with more education.

Three of my course mates were determined to make a go out of it and start a business. They wanted to set up a studio and workshop and they kindly invited me to join them in this venture.

But I wasn't sure it was right for me.

Part of me felt there was something else I needed to do.

After University, while the plan took some time to develop, we all returned to our hometowns. I returned to Newcastle to live with my family and continued working part time in a Tesco Express supermarket. I was lucky enough I could keep the same part-time job I had at University. It gave me money and something to do, which I very much needed. It also gave me time to explore my options without the pressure of making any rash decisions. Part of me was really excited by the idea of self-employment and part of me was excited about joining a really cool company.

As the weeks went by and I escaped the bubble of University I had time to reflect. This was the first time in my life I had actually asked myself, "What do I really want to do with my life? Or at least, what do I want to do now? Where could I best apply my skills and talents? What opportunities could I create? What is there to do? What kind of environment do I want to work in? What kind of company do I want to be part of?"

I started to think about some of the recent experiences I'd had alongside my academic educational journey.

• When I was seventeen, I took part in a personal leadership programme that took me to India. I climbed a mountain in the Himalayas, and I was inspired. I was encouraged to do something incredible with my life and to go and make a difference.

• At University I spent one summer in an American Summer Camp, teaching sports and activities in the great outdoors. I loved the developmental aspect of working with young people and inspiring them to be the best they could be.

• At University I was paid to give tours around the campus, a job I loved because I got to talk a lot and be generally positive and helpful.

• In my slightly younger years, I was a football coach. Again a job I loved because I got to teach. Something that was in my family's nature.

All of these experiences circulated in my mind. They all involved a mix of working with people, inspiring and problem solving. I tried to connect the dots and decide how I could apply all of these skills. How could I do something that would let me do what I was best at? Even though I didn't quite know what it was? As much as I loved designing and making things, I knew it wasn't exactly what I was put on this earth to do.

*

This way or that way. Forwards or standing still. I felt like I was in the middle of a game of chess and it was my turn to move. I had a depleted board and the only move I could really make would put me in a worse situation. This decision to join my friends on this business venture was getting to me. All I could think and say was "I don't know" and all I could feel was "it doesn't feel right".

There was a definite voice inside of me that was calling the adventure of self-employment, I did want to do my own thing. The idea of being entrepreneurial was intriguing.

I'd grown up listening to stories about choices my family had made, with some stories leaving the impression that chances weren't taken or risk wasn't fully encouraged. People doing what they were pressurised into, opposed to following their hearts, or taking the safe option instead of the one that really lit them up.

In some instances the ones that were comfortable and relatively well paid, but not exciting. I wanted exciting. My Mum on the other hand, had quite a few jobs. Jobs that combined what she loved and what she was really good at; first, a learning mentor for students with educational and behavioural challenges, gradually working up to the management and training of adults in social care.

The experiences I had and joy I got from teaching and development jobs were enough to cast doubt over me continuing the design route. I knew deep down I had to let this manufactured dream go. I had to do my own thing.

But with so much friendship and promised fun attached to this opportunity, I couldn't. I continued the 'I need to think about it' card. Clearly just delaying what should have been a difficult but honest conversation.

We all agreed to let the ship wait in the harbour a little longer.

Selfishly, I was desperate to find something else to make this a clear choice. I wanted to find something so much better, so I could say no to my friends with a rationale to cover the real reason I wasn't going to join their business venture. I just didn't want to. It didn't feel right.

I created an internship opportunity with a design agency in London. I worked hard to win a small design competition but the internship only lasted four weeks because my personal values got in the way. I didn't agree with a big project they had with an online gambling firm. I thought to myself "do I want to help make people's gambling experience better online?" I said no to myself and left. I was back where I started.

But now I was back with a real indication that I didn't want to follow this path of being a designer. I was more confident to say no, but actually saying it petrified me. Saying no would leave me on my own to figure things out. It wasn't the difficult conversation that terrified me, but the aftermath, the consequences of walking away. I felt secure by having an available avenue – even if it wasn't one I was excited by.

The anxiety was starting to build as I knew I had nothing to mask the decision to say no. A decision I'd magnified to become hugely significant. I told story after story in my mind. I painted vivid pictures of what saying 'yes' would look like and what 'no' would leave me with. I hated both options. What is worse, pursing a path I didn't believe in or having no plan at all?

Saying no to this opportunity meant leaving behind everything I'd worked for over the last four years and seeing my good friends skip off to a new life without me. I suddenly realised I was making this all about me. I couldn't face being alone. Being disconnected. Having nothing but a part-time job in a supermarket to show for my achievements. But most importantly, no plan, no purpose and nothing to strive towards. I knew I was being extremely selfish. I couldn't bare it.

One Thursday at work in Tesco's, I returned to the staff room on my lunch break and took my phone from my jacket pocket. I had a missed call and voicemail. The words 'you have one new message' sent shivers through me and took my breath. In my limbo of indecision, I'd allowed my friends and business partners to-be, to believe I was with them on this venture. I took advantage of their kind and patient nature.

They were looking for a house in Sheffield for us to live in. It would be the base for our business and they were calling me to share the excitement. My body flooded with anxiety. My hands sweated. My breath got faster and faster. I didn't know what was happening. I felt out of control.

I had my first panic attack. In a matter of seconds, it felt like the world stopped and the only thing that was moving was me. Like I was being spun around and shaken to wake up and do something to stop it.

Every cell in my body knew I couldn't go through with it. In a state of panic, I returned the call. I made the only logical excuse I could think of.

"I think it's too expensive and I'm going to need more time to save some money."

The house even had an apple tree in the garden, it sounded amazing. For a moment, as I pictured the apple tree, the scales nearly tipped in the other direction. But I said the time wasn't right. I said no.

I could breathe again. It was all going to be okay for at least another week or so. I could return to my moderately filled, anxious resting place.

I could return to my resting place with manageable anxiety.

Chapter 2

# LETTING GO

"When you say yes to others,
make sure you are not saying no to yourself"

Paulo Coelho

A month later it happened again. I'd been given an ultimatum to get off the fence and say yes or no. I had four sleepless nights in a row. I desperately searched for reasons to say yes. By now I was so confused by what was real and what I'd conjured up in my mind, I just wanted it all to go away. I thought if I found a way to say yes I could definitely make it all go away.

I couldn't handle the pain.

In a state of sheer panic and desperation, I did two memorable things. The first was to get hypnotised. I thought I'd be able to get to the bottom of the crazy space I was in and be able to say "yes" to this decision. I paid around £60 and the conversation went something like this…

"I have a big decision to make and I'm struggling to say yes. I think I want to do it. I'm not sure if I'm scared or just don't want to. Can you help me?"

30 minutes later, after a very tranquil experience of hypnosis, I woke up. I felt a little calmer but no differently about my decision. The only thing that really changed was I was £60 worse off! I went home.

The second memorable encounter was two nights later, after a midnight panic attack.

I woke up in a cold sweat, my mind was racing and I couldn't breathe. I was spiralling out of control. I didn't know what to do or who could help me. My parents were asleep in the other room and I didn't want to wake them, but I desperately needed help.

Without thinking too much, I called the Samaritans - a service that provides confidential emotional support for people who are experiencing feelings of distress, despair or suicidal thoughts. I'd never called them before but it felt like the only place I could turn.

My hands shook as I dialled the number.

"I need some help…"

"Are you suicidal?"

No.

"Are you sure?"

"Yes. I just need to make a decision that's tearing me up. I'm hurting a lot. I'm scared and I don't know what to do.."

In between hyperventilating, I explained how I felt and the operator kindly reassured me that it was all going to be okay.

The rest of the night I can't remember what happened. After the shock of the panic, I must have fallen asleep.

*

The next evening came quickly, my good friend Ric came round to my house, one of the three friends I was planning to move to Sheffield with. We'd been best friends for the previous four years, after living and studying together.

He brought the paperwork to sign for the house. It was an amazing house in a really nice part of Sheffield, but sadly with no apple tree. It was like a golden ticket and my opportunity to get my independence back. Living at home had the pleasantries of a full fridge and all the mod cons that students manage to live without, but it was nothing compared to the freedom of living on your own.

My Mum and Dad stood by my side, offering supporting as always. Support being, if financially I needed help, they'd be there, but more importantly, words to the effect of "We believe in you. We know this is a little scary, but do it."

I smiled a forced smile. I signed the paper. I was doing it. The ball was in motion.

I said "I'll see you soon!" with fake excitement.

I went to bed.

*

As you can imagine, I didn't sleep very well. This decision I'd made did not come from my instinct, my gut, my heart or any higher guidance. It came from fear. Fear that I'd have to face the music of my own decisions. Fear that I couldn't hide behind anyone else's dreams. Fear of being alone. Fear of being exposed. Fear of having to be fully in control. Fear of being lost.

It was like something telling me this wasn't my choice.

*

The next morning, Ric was leaving to go to Sheffield to finalise the paperwork.

I woke up at 7 am with a surge of energy from my stomach. I knew I had to stop this. I'd been so scared, to tell the truth. I'd been pushed so close to what I didn't want, that I finally found the conviction I needed.

I got in my Mum's car before she needed it to go to work and drove the ten-minute journey to Ric's house. I needed to catch him before he set off on the train. Everything inside of me started to scream. But this time it came from my stomach, not the whirlwind of my mind.

I arrived at his house to find he was already on the train, so I had to call him. What I thought was going to be a difficult conversation was finally so easy because I had so little energy left in me.

"I'm outside your house. I came round to tell you I can't go through with it. I'm really sorry. I've been so scared to let this go, but it just really isn't right for me…"

27

"It's okay, don't worry. We'll figure something out. Thanks for letting us know. It's all going to be alright".

As I expected, Ric reassured me it was going to be okay. He sensed my uncertainty and fear. I knew deep down, that him and the others would be okay with my decision, they just needed to know.

I sat in the car for a few minutes to catch my breath. But still feeling a bit lost and ashamed, I dragged my depressed self out of the car and went in to see his Mum and Dad. Their comfort was much needed. I was a shadow of the person they knew. The outgoing, confident, cheerful Andy had been spun around into oblivion and left a confused mess.

After a brief conversation, I went home and collapsed on my bed. I was exhausted beyond anything I'd ever experienced, but I'd finally let go. I was beginning to surrender.

*

The lesson I was slowly learning reminded me of the first time learnt to water-ski.

As part of being a camp counsellor at Summer Camp, we were encouraged to take part in all of the activities with the campers. Water sports were way outside my comfort zone and I was about to water-ski for the first time.

As the boat slowly pulled away, I followed the instructions: I kept my arms strong and allowed the rope to pull me up as the board created friction against the water. In a matter of seconds, I was on the water. And in a split second, I fell forwards and my face smashed into the water. This is where you let go of the rope and start again.

But instead of letting go, my instinctive fight or flight response told me to hold on - hold on to a speedboat dragging me through the water with skis on! Ouch indeed. This was the most painful four seconds my arms have ever experienced. What was I thinking? I wasn't - I just panicked and held on for dear life. I quickly realised you need to let go to keep your life going! The expression should be, let go for dear life!

I strained muscles in my arms and my shoulders. The pain served as a constant reminder for about four days. I got the message: let go.

*

It was still only 8 am and my parents were about to go to work.

The feelings were still getting worse. I'd held on to this decision for so long that I'd drained my body with so much nervous energy. I googled the word depression to find a definition, it translated to mean 'nervous exhaustion' - it made a lot of sense.

I told my Mum the decision I'd made before she went to work. Stood on the landing outside her bedroom I broke down in tears. I cried in front of her for the first time. They were partly tears of a genuine emotional breakdown and partly manufactured to indicate to her how desperately I needed someone to help me.

She comforted me but had to go to work so said we could talk about it later.

So this is where you let go and sit still. You breathe; you sit down and take one hour at a time. You don't make rash decisions, you don't panic.

But I was still in panicked and confused mode. I felt a wave of fear and regret wash over me. My whole body was alert and troubled by the feeling of making the wrong decision. I felt lost, alone and vulnerable. It was the first time I'd made a big decision that I thought was the right thing to do. But because I was in the middle of an anxious breakdown, it didn't feel like I'd made the right choice. Let alone could I be patient enough to let some time unfold.

I wanted to get my decision back. I didn't understand why it hurt so much. I was alone in terms of being the only person in the house, but more so in a spiritually disconnected sense.

I decided to get a train to Sheffield.

I took a bus to the train station and asked when the next train was. I had 15 minutes to buy a ticket and drag myself on board. To any passer-by, there would be no indication of the mental state I was in. No signs that my mind was swirling at one hundred miles an hour. No, sign that I felt scared about my future. And no signs I was in the aftermath of a nervous breakdown.

I waited and stood completely still until the train was ready to depart. I wasn't getting on. I called my Mum at work and told her where I was, what I was trying to do.

"Mum, I'm at the train station. I tried to get on a train to Sheffield but I'm stuck and can't do it. I think I need to see you."

Being the World's Greatest Mum, she asked me to come and meet her outside her work. She took me inside for coffee and soup, it was probably the most I'd ever needed a hug.

Together we decided, I was very depressed and I needed help.

Chapter 3

# ON MY OWN

"Rock bottom became the solid
foundation from which I built my life"

- J.K. Rowling

It was St Patrick's Day. I'd just collected my anti-depressants from the chemist. Newcastle, being a city that loves to celebrate any event that involves drinking alcohol, was in full flow - Guinness hats were everywhere as people joined in the Irish national holiday.

I was walking back from the doctor's and, as if by chance, I bumped into a good friend called Peter. Apart from looking slightly tired, there was no obvious indication I was in a bad place. He asked me if I'd like to have a drink.

"Shall we go for a quick pint of Guinness?"

"Actually, I'm having a bad time at the moment. I've just been to doctors. I'm depressed so I need to go home and take these pills and be on my own for a little while, sorry."

That would have been the overtly honest thing to say and do. But instead, I obliged and went for a pint.

As you can imagine, I wasn't great conversation. I battled through a token pint of Guinness and went home to be depressed. I got into bed, wrapped myself in covers and stayed as still as possible until somebody spoke to me. Apart from drinking water to take the nasty tasting medication, I didn't eat or drink anything else all day.

This was a place I really didn't expect to be.

*

On day one of admitting I was depressed, I had no idea how to describe how I felt. And more worryingly I had no idea what I needed to do to make myself better. I didn't know how to navigate through the miserable landscape in my mind.

I never felt like I needed help with emotional issues or psychological things. I wasn't sure if other men or people my age did that, or if it was just me that resisted it.

This was the first time in my life I felt like I actually needed to be helped in this kind of way. Thankfully, when I was pulled to my knees, crying helplessly, I had support. I had my mum there to catch me when I fell. My Mum wasn't a qualified counsellor or therapist and she didn't intend to treat me. But what she did do was make me feel okay with not being okay. And she made me feel it was courageous and brave to ask for help.

Before I fully crashed, I'd already been through a traumatic and emotional journey. My anxiety had caused my life to spill out into a confused mess around me. I'd called emergency services, I had panic attacks, sleepless nights and I was almost unable to function. Had I known reaching out for help earlier was an option, I would have saved myself a lot of pain and suffering.

I learnt that it's okay not to be okay, but not necessary to suffer alone.

I needed to get help. I needed to be courageous enough to make the first step and accept the support available.

*

Getting help for depression was a fairly straightforward process. I told my GP I was depressed and I got drugs to make me feel okay.

I got home later that afternoon and got back into bed. I took the horrible tasting medication and slowly pondered what was happening. How long would it take for me to feel okay? What had I done to deserve this pain? What would make it go away?

For some people, anti-depressants are an important first step to regulating mood and bringing people into the kind of emotional state where they can function to a good degree. For other people, they can do more damage. People become dependent on them and never believe or try to live another way. For me, I didn't think they should be a long-term solution and fundamentally I didn't agree with medicating my way through life unless I absolutely needed to. I didn't want to take what I considered at the time, to be the easy way out.

After a few days of taking them, I stopped and reconsidered. I thought if I wasn't born needing drugs to regulate my mood, something or a collection of things in my life had brought me to a place where I was in need. But I didn't want to be in need of drugs, I wanted a more natural approach.

After a few days of staying in bed (until my parents got home to cook me dinner) and being sick of taking pills that I didn't understand - I went back to the doctor's to discuss other forms of treatment. I had very little understanding of mental health issues, but my instinct told me that medication wasn't the answer.

In school, we were taught the difference between mental health and mental illness, but it's the kind of class you attend and never think you'll need to know the information. I really did want to know. I wanted to know everything.

After understanding my wish to stop taking medication, the Doctor offered to enrol me into Cognitive Behavioural Therapy (CBT). CBT is a process of talking with a therapist to understand the nature of my thoughts and it could help me overcome my problems by changing the way I think. It sounded much more like the right thing to me, compared to putting chemicals into my body to mask the pain. I wanted to understand what the problem was and make a solution. Problem-solving was my thing. But the problem was somewhere lost in the circuitry of my mind and manifested itself as a chemical mix-up. My mum thought I had a hormone imbalance. And I definitely did. But I felt I'd created it myself or at least made it a lot worse.

The doctor signed me up for CBT. A huge relief - but not immediately helpful. I was put on a six-month waiting list! Six months felt like an eternity. I wanted help now. If you have an exciting holiday booked to Disneyland, a six-month wait is usually part of the excitement. But when you are desperately trying to figure out why your life feels a mess, it's a different ball game altogether.

This was almost enough to tip me back over the edge. What I really wanted, was to talk to someone who knew what had happened to me. I wanted to be told everything was going to be okay, preferably with some instructions as to what to do about it. Or a magic wand to make it all better, but that was probably too much to ask.

I really wanted to get on and do stuff. Not twiddle my thumbs for six months and wait to have a conversation that I didn't even know would help.

Instead of asking myself "what's wrong with me?" I wanted to be told I was going to be okay. Instead of feeling alone, I wanted to know I had support. And instead of wondering how I'd possibly recover, I wanted a plan.

I decided to take matters into my own hands.

As I'd made the confident step to stop taking the medication, I felt it was up to me to understand how to make myself better.

*

A few weeks later, I managed to drag myself out of bed. I was walking past the book section in a supermarket and came across a book by Paul McKenna, a self-help hypnotherapist. The promise on the front of the book was "I Can Make You Happy". Even though depression is a very different ball game to sadness, I definitely wasn't happy and it was a good place to start.

This was my introduction to the world of self-help. At the time, reading really wasn't my favourite thing to be doing. I hadn't read books out of choice for years. I read a couple at University for my dissertation, but never out of choice. One of the reasons I pursued a more vocational route for further education was because I didn't enjoy sitting and reading. I much preferred to make things.

Paying attention long enough to read full books was a skill I hadn't yet mastered. But in this instance, I wanted to find answers way more than I hated sitting down to read.

Little did I know, this would be a turning point to me becoming a reading enthusiast! Necessity would become a great motivator.

*

Over the next few months, I decided that the best thing I could do was to get myself better. The outside world could wait until my inside world was smiling again. Plans for inspiring work and changing the world in my own little way were on hold.

I wanted to really understand why this had happened to me. I became fascinated with my own mind and how I ended up in such a muddle. The incident that caused the downward thought spiral could have been anything, it just so happened to be a life decision about whether to relocate cities and join a business venture.

More importantly, I wanted to understand the way I dealt with it. I guessed it was just a reflection of my nature. A magnified explosion of my thought process: the anxiety, indecision, overthinking and occasional impulsiveness. The roller coaster of emotions I rode was incredible. I felt moments of mania that I didn't know I was capable of and periods of despair I'd hate to relive. It was a very frightening time, but if I could use this as an enlightening learning experience, it could change the rest of my life.

That's what I set out to do.

*

When you begin a journey of introspection, you have to be willing to question and challenge deep parts of your character and personality. Importantly, you have to want to change something. I began to think back to the personal effectiveness course I went on whilst in Sixth Form College. One of the greatest skills we were taught was how to reflect on your own experiences - to highlight the things that were positive, to learn from mistakes and to not let the negative things happen again.

But this was a huge thing I was trying to understand, or at least I'd made it a huge thing. I wanted to meet a psychologist or neuroscientist and get to the heart of what was going on. I wanted to understand myself better; my inner mind, the gifts I was born with and the innate challenges that came with them. I turned to self-awareness and turned myself into a project to study.

*

Solving problems that you can see is a lot easier than solving ones you can't. Seeing my situation as a problem wasn't necessarily a correct assessment, but it did motivate me to get better as quickly as I could. I like problems and I liked learning.

My first port of call was to diagnose the problem with a little help from Google. As self-proclaiming organisers of the world's information, they make mental health research and self-diagnosis very easy, perhaps too easy.

I thought it was difficult to explain to other people what was going inside my mind – it's far easier to go on Google and find some symptoms or an illness that closely matched what I 'thought' was wrong with me.

I decided blaming my mind would be a good place to start. I started to dig into the causes of anxiety and how it affects people's lives. I started to connect all of the dots from my behaviour in education, in work and in my life. Of course, I found a lot of good examples and stories to support this self-fulfilling prophecy.

I needed things to make sense.

I started to see my boundless creativity and poor attention as part of the problem. I wasn't trying to be negative about myself; I knew

I was in a lot of ways very gifted and talented. But I did desperately want a label to hide behind.

Aside from spending my time diagnosing lots of problems, I was very proactive in seeking external help. I joined a life-coaching group called Life Club. They met every Tuesday night and worked through exercises to help people overcome personal challenges they were having in their lives. I was really into it for a few weeks. But because all of the other group members were slightly older women, I felt a little separate on my journey. I couldn't fully empathise with their situations and I wasn't sure they could with mine either.

It was a really valuable and supportive group, it just happened to be not quite what I needed at the time.

*

A few months had passed and I was at the train station again. But this time I was getting on.

It was 8 am on a Tuesday morning and I was excited for a day trip to Stratford Upon Avon, a 10-hour round trip. I was going for an assessment with a company called Dore - an amazing company that supports adults with learning difficulties, particularly with ADD (Attention Deficit Disorder) and Dyslexia. The best part about their approach is that they don't label or diagnose people with a problem or a disorder. Instead, they give you a learning programme with daily activities that will improve the parts of the brain that need to be more efficient.

In my research, I decided that I may have undiagnosed ADD, ADHD or Dyslexia and this could be one of the amplifiers to my problematic circumstances.

If you are wondering why I decided to travel half the length of the country for an assessment when I could have a different one in my home town, I'd say it felt like my only option. My impulsive and hyper-focused nature made it seem like it was what I had to do. I bought into their approach, of not diagnosing.

I was certain I had ADD. I'd overcome the immediate period of depression and I was starting to find a life plan. But I couldn't let this go. I really wanted to understand how and why I do the things I do. "Why I am so creative? Why am I able to vividly imagine complex ideas so quickly? Why do I struggle to make decisions and love to invent more and more ways to do things? Why do I misplace so many things and leave a trail of belongings everywhere I go? Why do allow my mind to take over my life? And why do I suffer from anxiety?"

I arrived at the Dore Centre and I was ready for my assessment. It began with a question and answer session and was followed by a series of cognitive tests, balance tests, and eye tests.

Whatever the result turned out to be, I was having a great time!

This kind of place appealed to my inner geek of curiosity and inspired my new-found passion for understanding how people learn, think and behave.

The assessment gave real-time feedback, so I didn't have to go away and wait for a conclusion. And, importantly, it wasn't a case of passing or failing, like a driving test. It was an assessment of how my brain was currently functioning.

But in the excitement of the trip, I forgot they were never going to say "you have ADD" - that wasn't their approach. Their approach was to provide a personal development plan. A plan mostly comprising of physical exercises to effectively rewire parts of the brain. Their approach was not to give people a golden envelope with an excuse. But give people an actual way of living a better quality life.

I was torn in how I felt. Part of me thought, "Wow, this is incredible, what a positive way to approach things. What an amazing company. Sign me up. Let's do it." The other part of me was disappointed. I wanted to be able to tell people the depression, anxiety, panic attacks and my nervous breakdown all happened because I have ADD. And people with ADD find x thing difficult.

This wasn't what I wanted.

*

Before I left the centre, we made an outline of a development plan that I could follow, complete with online learning and daily exercises that would be tailored exactly to me. It sounded incredible. But the only problem was it was relatively expensive. At least for a University graduate who decided earning money wasn't a priority.

I was earning just enough money to live and pay my bills, but I'd chosen to work as little as possible to give me more time to figure things out. A month later I'd committed to a conference in America so I had to turn down the programme because I didn't have enough money. Being truthful, I didn't need more debt. But the real reason I said no was I didn't want to do all of the hard work required.

Saying yes to the programme would mean accepting that there wasn't really a problem at all - just some things I needed to do, to manage my mind better. A few daily exercises and perhaps learning to meditate. It was a matter of accepting who I am and doing the things I needed to do.

I had an ice cream served from a novelty narrow boat on the river and headed back to the train station.

It was time to go home and put this quest for finding excuses behind me, I started being proactive with my life.

Chapter 4

# THE SEARCH

"If you haven't found it yet, keep looking.
As with all matters of the heart
you'll know when you find it"

- Steve Jobs

I was free at last. Free from walking in the shadows of other people's dreams. And free from finding problems that would justify my situation. It was time to be proactive with my life.

This chapter is where I find my thing to do. A time to put introspection on hold and find happiness in meaningful work and in the world outside of myself.

I was pretty open to trying anything and determined to do something to keep my life moving forward. Whilst previously I was set on finding the perfect next career and life step, it was time for more doing and less thinking.

\*

I loved the city of Newcastle, but I wanted to find a way to leave. I wasn't comfortable being back here. My old friends weren't particularly interested in the things I was, (though I couldn't articulate it at the time) and as much as I love my family, I needed to spread my wings. I felt limited. I felt isolated in a place I thought was home.

I thought the quicker I found my path, the quicker I could be successful and the quicker I'd actually be happy. I'd be able to prove all my education was worth it and prove I was making the right life choices.

I was driven, but I needed to be patient. I felt like I had to sacrifice something, I couldn't have it all, at least straight away. I wanted my independence back, but I wasn't prepared to pay for it, at least not with a job that wasn't fulfilling.

I decided I wanted time. I wanted time and flexibility more than I wanted money and therefore my independence. Time to try things, time to search, time to explore, in the hope I'd stumble across what I was looking for.

I decided to stay living with my parents for a while. Their patience and kindness were such a blessing, I am so grateful they supported me as I figured things out.

What was I looking for?As I sat and dreamt beyond the walls of my bedroom, Mum gave me a song to listen to. The words helped describe how I felt about my current situation and life ahead of me.

The song is called 'I Can Be Astonishing' by Rebecca Wicking. It was as if both Rebecca Wicking and my mum were both saying to me, "it's all going to be okay, there is a wonderful life waiting for you". The song itself, was one of many songs that gave me a vital sense of perspective and a much needed boost.

*

One day everything changed.

I continued my part time job in my local Tesco store. I made enough money to live the basic lifestyle I chose and could save a little bit extra. It was conveniently close to where I was living, which meant I didn't have to spend any money travelling and I could work in a flexible way which meant I could do other things.

I was working with a friend called Laura – a textile design student and a lover of life's creative journey. She'd helped me win the design competition a year earlier that led me to the internship in London (the one I ended up quitting). Whilst that hadn't lead me to the place I wanted, it was learning experience and helped us become good friends.

As we spent a lot of time together, she got to know me and kindly listened as I expressed my overlapping interests in design, business, and general problem solving.

Then one day she opened a door for me.

A friend of hers had stumbled upon a management approach called 'service design' or 'design thinking' – a relatively new approach to consultancy, which apparently had my name written all over it. Trusting Laura's judgment, I went home to read about it.

I didn't know much about the consultancy industry at all, but after a quick Google search, I got very excited. It sounded like something I could do. It seemed creative enough, complex enough and something new, which made it all the more appealing.

I wanted to find the quickest way to learn a lot about it.

Not doing things by halves I decided to volunteer at a conference on the other side of the world. A conference that attracted thought leaders and speakers from some of the world's leading companies. This was the America trip I mentioned in the previous chapter.

I contacted the conference organiser in Berlin and passionately relayed my newfound interest in this growing discipline, my ability to be super helpful for the conference delegates and indicating I had some knowledge of San Francisco (I'd been for three days.) I had just enough money to pay for my flight and a hostel for four nights.

I was on my way to San Francisco.

As I boarded the plane and set off on this journey, all of my other worries were left behind. In the presence of an exciting opportunity, all of my previous worries seemed to melt away. I hoped a little boldness would return some good fortune, as sitting at home wasn't really working.

I jumped on a plane full of enthusiasm and hope. I was open to learning and ready to be the best conference organiser I could be.

*

A day later I arrived in a hostel in San Francisco where 25 other volunteers would be staying. I was greeted my some of the nicest, most interesting and fun people I'd ever met. Something instantly clicked and I knew this trip was going to be amazing.

I met people that loved to learn. People that wanted to advance thinking in this area of business and innovation. People that were leaders in their own right from all over the world. And I met people so giving they would share everything they'd already learnt with me. I wasn't quite sure it was real but it felt amazing. It was a world away from home or anything I'd experienced before. It was like I was living a second life.

We spent our days being fully immersed in the seminars and speaking events. We participated in all of the workshops and we were able to input our own thoughts and ideas. I felt heard and valued.

All I had to do in return was wear a branded t-shirt and be helpful. It was definitely time well spent and an opportunity with many potential benefits.

I could dream way beyond the limits of my hometown and connect new ideas. It was like new parts of my brain were lighting up, new visions of what I could do were being ignited - a new me was evolving.

*

After four days of learning and being part of something special - I had to go back to England.

I returned home with more than I could have possibly hoped for. I had a job opportunity in Atlanta, an invitation to kick-start an event in my hometown and a pile of business cards from people I could contact for work opportunities.

But more important than all of those things - I had my sense of purpose back. I had a new vision for where my life and work could take me. I had new friends I felt connected too. I had a spring in my step – I was bursting with energy. I'd unlocked a whole world of possibilities. It was definitely my thing.

Seeing so many other ex-designers transitioning to another kind of work was liberating. The instinct I had that my skillset shouldn't go to waste was proving to be true. I didn't have to restrict the way I applied my love for problem-solving and creating things. I met people tackling social challenges, improving business operations, customer experience specialists and people being generally entrepreneurial. The shackles were off. I was free from the narrow and limiting box I'd painted around myself.

I found new people for this phase of my life. I was beginning to realise that our friendship groups can and should evolve as we do.

The friendships I struggled so hard to let go of, suddenly made sense to me. My heart quietly poured with anguish, thinking I had caused so much unnecessary pain for others. Thankfully, they were wonderfully forgiving friends and it was all okay.

University was the first time I'd met people that were as equally inspired and passionate about the things I was; people that were fascinated by exact measures, ergonomic angles and being generally experimental. It didn't matter what we were doing; we connected because we cared about similar things. I had the same experience all over again. Now I wanted to be around people that were going to be innovative leaders. People that were going to challenge conventional business approaches and people that wanted to use their creativity for good.

I arrived home and lay down. I began to process the little big adventure I'd just been on. Little, as it was only five days and big, because it was hugely transformative.

\*

My horizon had well and truly shifted. From the confines of my hometown to an open world full of possibilities. My life plans were starting to take shape. I felt inspired.

I thought back to the moment I walked away from my previous path in chapter one. The moment I let go. The road that was beginning to unfold in front of me was only possible because I found the conviction to walk away from something I didn't truly want to do.

With a little bit of perspective, I reflected on the importance of listening to my heart, especially in big decisions where passion is involved. Going through a dramatic and emotional decision-making process gave me a huge wake-up call. It was as if someone was screaming at me to listen to my intuition - instead of following through with something I clearly didn't want to do.

Deciding whether to follow my friends in a business venture and relocate cities was difficult. I was obsessed with making the right choice. I felt so much pressure to make the perfect decision and not let other people down in the process. As I thought through the different options ahead of me, my mind raced forward making elaborate plans that were impossible to comprehend. And the more I thought about it, the more frightened I became.

The decision I wanted to make was within me all along, it was just clouded by fear and postponed by my lack of self-confidence. It gave me a shocking insight to how severe my levels of anxiety were. Holding on to something I didn't want to do, not only made me suffer unnecessary pain, but it also prevented me from finding what I did want. While I was focused on hiding the tension I felt inside me, I was closed off to any possible good things happening.

It also taught me to be more respectful of other people's feelings and plans, but not to sacrifice my own happiness in the process. While I was so wrapped up in what I wanted to do, I lost perspective of being fair and empathetic to people I was inadvertently affecting. Having respect for them and having an honest conversation, was in the end much more helpful than ignoring the matter and thinking they'd be somehow offended.

In this instance, I had to get close to what I didn't want to do before I found the conviction to admit how I really felt and tell my friends I didn't want to go ahead with it. Thankfully, they were very understanding and let me get on with what I needed to do. Once I wasn't involved, they were able to do what they needed to do and make their life happen. Which turned out wonderfully well.

The next six months I felt like I was living a second life. I spent two days a week in my part time job in Tesco and the rest of my time furiously learning.

Previously it took immense willpower to motivate me for this part-time job. Now, instead of thinking "I am better than this" – I realised that this was exactly the place I needed to be. I swapped resentment for gratitude. I found new meaning in what I recently felt was "just a part-time job". Instead of feeling I only had things to take from my work, I learnt to give something instead.

It suddenly became okay because I had a sense of something else to work towards. I could love being a customer service assistant for a couple of days a week. And I could skip home excited about what I'd be reading or the plans in store for the following day.

By having a bigger purpose, I found a way to be grateful for the job I had and the situation I was in. I realised how quickly opportunities could arise if we are open to seeing them. And I also realised that some opportunities are presented to us but it's up to us if we take them.

This conference was just the beginning.

I was starting to see a path I had to walk down.

Chapter 5

# LEAPS OF FAITH

"Do not go where the path may lead,
go instead where there is no path and leave a trail"

- Ralph Waldo Emerson

New opportunities arose but the core of my being was still uneasy. There was a feeling of emptiness I was desperate to hide. If you probed me about my sense of personal peace, you'd find something was missing.

I didn't give it any attention at all. Instead, I threw myself into lots of new opportunities. I had a new wave of momentum behind me, I couldn't let it go to waste.

The anxiety about my career plans had faded. I had my zest for life back and a new subject to study. I was a beginner again. This new outlook on my life empowered me and gave me a sense of control, at least with regards to my career path.

My newly open-mindedness about how my career was going to unfold was largely due to one conversation. At the internship that I decided to walk away from, I did learn something that changed what I thought it meant to "make a living".

I'd just graduated University and I was still deciding on the one thing I wanted to do with my life. I was looking for the one job that would fulfil all of my interests and allow me to do work that mattered. At the agency, I met one of the freelance team. I was very new to the marketing world and keen to meet people.

"So what do you do then?"

"I'm a part-time web developer. So I help out big projects when they don't have enough people in-house."

"Ah cool. So what do you do when you are not a web developer?"

"I'm a stunt man."

I looked at him at if he'd said something rude or really out of context. He repeated it to help my brain send a message to my puzzled face to say it's okay.

"I'm a stunt man. I impersonate premiership footballers on TV adverts. Like doing overhead kicks for Nike adverts and things like that."

At first, the penny didn't drop. But as any footballing fan would in this situation I unleashed the can of worms to know more about this amazing job. I guess I knew this kind of job must exist and people must do them, but you don't normally meet people who do it. Or at least I didn't.

In one conversation, all of my previous beliefs about having one job disappeared.

1) You don't just have to do one thing; you can have multiple passions and get paid for doing it (providing you can balance your life and make it work).

2) You can get paid to do things you totally love doing. The word job has mixed connotations and doesn't often conjure up images of people being stunt men. While we can't all be stunt men, we can choose to find work that excites us, and get paid for it.

I knew the days of having the same job for life were long gone and people will change jobs or careers throughout their lives, but I didn't know I could do two at once! Or that work could be that much fun!

It didn't really sink in at the time. I think I was just really impressed that I met a stunt man.

*

I came back to Newcastle, feeling totally energised. I followed up job opportunities and leads from the conference in America. I turned down a job opportunity in Atlanta to be an innovation consultant specialising in retail. I wasn't crazy about the idea of Atlanta, although I had a lot of retail experience, it wasn't where I wanted to specialise. I surprised myself with how quickly I was able to say no.

I then applied for a job in Oslo with a really cool design and innovation agency. Even though I was slightly nervous of the lifestyle there, the possibility of great projects excited me more than I was afraid of it. But I didn't get it. My degree didn't reflect the necessary skillset I needed, or at least, I didn't know how to express the skills I'd gained in a way they understood and saw valuable. I was struggling to see past the end products I'd made, and so were the people I was applying for jobs with.

After this demoralising rejection letter, I decided to change tactic. An opportunity came up to deliver a weekend training event called Global Service Jam. It was organised by a small consultancy firm in Germany but delivered by volunteers all over the world. The intention was to help promote an exciting and new approach to business innovation.

Deep down I loved the idea of doing my own thing; this was an opportunity to try it. We would have the creative freedom to lead and manage the event, but still have support if we needed it. It was a freeing chance to put everything into practice that I'd been learning over the past few months.

I contacted two of the event volunteers I met in San Francisco and persuaded them to come to Newcastle so we could run it together. Louise lived in London and Neils lived in Copenhagen.

I was inspired to do it, we all were. Like the opportunity was pulling us forward. We knew at some point we had to create our own opportunities. But I was also scared beyond belief.

Thankfully, Louise helped me over the edge of my fear. As soon as we registered to do it, it all came together. We found a venue, marketed the event and planned the two-day programme. Everything was ready, apart from my Mum.

At the time, I was still living with my parents - which I was extremely grateful for. But as I made plans I unthinkingly invited Louise and Neils to stay with me in Newcastle, expecting it would be okay - as it had never been a problem before. But to my Mum, my two new good friends were practically strangers. I'd only met them once and all of a sudden I was claiming we'd somehow "connected" and I trusted them.

There was no way on earth they were going to stay.

At first, I couldn't understand. I thought my Mum was being awkward and would eventually give in to my charm and persuasion. But she didn't budge.

"They can stay in a hotel. We'll find one nearby". Mum insisted.

This really wasn't part of my plan. We were running a voluntary event to help kick-start our careers and they were travelling from London and Copenhagen. I didn't want them to have to pay extra expenses of hotels on top of flights and trains. The least we could do was offer them a place to stay.

My Mum is lovely and wonderful. This wasn't about how kind or giving she wanted to be. She was so supportive of everything I did. But the idea of this was making her really uncomfortable.

I sat with her, to try and talk about it. It was the first time I'd been aware enough to see the anxiety in someone else. It was as if someone was holding up a mirror to show me how I cope with anxiety.

My mum broke down into tears. I couldn't remember the last time I'd seen my mum cry. I hugged her and said I was sorry to have brought this on. But after all of the recent reading I'd done and the anxiety-training course I attended as part of my therapy, I was able to empathise with my mum. I could understand what she was thinking and where the fear was emanating from.

I did my best to compassionately explain that it was all going to be okay.

It was a huge step outside what my mum was comfortable with. Given her upbringing and life experiences, she was right to feel nervous – and I had to understand that. Thankfully I managed it and they both stayed. We all had a really good time - a huge relief to my Dad and I because we thought we were causing more trouble than it was worth. I hoped this would be a little turning point or a learning point at least for my mum. Because for me, it was a mini-breakthrough. Thanks, Mum.

It was so important I saw how Mum reacted and coped with this situation. It didn't matter what the situation was, but it showed me how we sometimes deal with fear. I knew that if I was going to progress in my life and work, I couldn't let fear stop me.

*

The three of us ran an incredible event, a first and a major confidence boost to all of us. We made a great team.

I'd not only found my thing, but I'd also lived through fear into a place of unexplainable joy. I knew I could get used to this kind of work. I'd figured out a way to merge my passions for teaching and coaching, with business and creativity. It was all very exciting.

Following this event, I took up theatrical improvisation to build on my facilitation skills. I'd never really heard of it before – someone at the event recommended I give it a try, so I did. It felt like other people were giving me signposts about which way to go and what to do. I had to listen and try things.

Following that, the mastermind team that organised Global Service Jam invited us, and all of the hosts to their headquarters in Germany to best practice with other innovation leaders. I was invited to teach an innovation course at Central St Martins University in London, I created work opportunities in Poland and Germany - slowly a purposeful path was opening up wonderfully.

I saw my future in a way I hadn't seen before.

Chapter 6

# CHASING SUCCESS

"Don't be too preoccupied with what is going
on around you. Pay more attention to what
it going on within you"

- Mary-Frances Winters

A few months passed. Opportunities came and went. A lot was happening in my life and I was grateful for how things were developing. I was connected to this new business and innovation world. But twice a week I was still working in a supermarket. I felt like I had a split identity. I knew something had to change.

I started to get slowly frustrated. I'd distracted myself with new career opportunities and for some time I forgot about where I was in the context of my career and life. I felt like I had so much potential to do great work, but nobody was letting me do it. Or at least, nobody was paying me to do it. I was bursting with ideas but I had no avenue to express myself. How was I going to start a career doing this kind of work?

I remember the five-minute walk home from work that day being filled with mixed emotions. I'd lost the feeling of gratitude, unable to be thankful that I actually had a job and I was being paid enough money to live, eat and pay my rent. I was twenty-four, I had a first class degree and some great experiences under my belt.

In my role as a customer service assistant, I started to get frustrated about the things I wasn't allowed to do. I started to look for problems and I found them.

I was frustrated: at the overly complicated procedures that meant every small problem had to be escalated to management, at the badly designed systems that wasted everyone's time, and - most importantly - that management targets were being prioritised over meeting the needs of customers. I felt like there was a huge disconnect between head office decision makers and the reality of what needed to happen for the best of everyone. I could hardly contain my anger.

As I write this now, I understand that this frustration was just a vehicle to express how I felt about where I was within myself. I wanted to be further ahead in my career and I wanted opportunities. But beneath that reasoning, I wanted the opportunities and success to hide my deeper insecurities.

Deep down my intention was good. I did know how to help, at least I thought I did. I was aware of commercially intelligent ways to make things more efficient. My newly educated perspective on the how businesses were evolving gave me some great insights and ideas.

But all of the goodness I had to offer was channelled through a filter of hate. I vented my frustration to my family, claiming I knew how to help to Tesco and make them lots of money. Money was what they seemed to care about.

I wanted to be heard and listened to.

Out of nowhere, misdirected rage was silenced by inspiration. I was sat at home in my room and accidently started watching a show called 'Undercover Boss'. A show that follows executives to the front line of their business, to see what really happens on a day-to-day basis. My mind raced with ideas and my feet filled with excitement.

I decided I could document all of my ideas and present them to the CEO. My blind optimism saw no flaws with this idea. I decided it would be a great way to start working with a really big company. The expression "go big or go home" came to mind. Seeing as I was already at home, I thought I might as well go big.

I relaxed. Everything was okay again. I had my sense of purpose back. I felt okay and excited by the situation I was in. I found a way to turn it around from being a victim with no opportunity, to an inspired individual with a way to change my life.

And so I did just that.

Although I was an employee of the company, I felt like I was representing something else. Like I was representing everyone on the front line of companies that wanted things to be different. People that wanted change to happen. I felt like the uniform was just a disguise - and there came an idea.

I was still labelling myself some kind of problem-solving designer, I decided to call myself a "Designer in Disguise". This little description totally empowered me. I thought it was a clever play on words, but more importantly, it gave me the inspiration and empowerment I needed at the time.

I found a way to channel all of my frustration in a positive way. I continued to give great service to each customer and use my lunch breaks to undertake this secret mission I was on. I scribbled away believing I was the eyes and ears of the CEO.

*

A week later the universe nudged me to change my life in a positive way.

I came across an opportunity to work on a government training programme called the National Citizen Service - a programme that encourages students from different backgrounds to mix together and develop social action projects to improve their communities. I'd be representing a youth organisation called Future Foundations.

This felt right up my street. Some of the previous experiences I'd had, suddenly made sense; the 3 months spent as a Camp Counsellor in America, the personal leadership programme I took part in and the many years I'd spend in sports coaching. The inner teacher in me had another opportunity to come out and play. And once again, it was someone else that recommended me for it.

As I contemplated taking this opportunity, I felt I was on the right path. The only hesitation was because I'd have to relocate to the South Coast of England. I needed to be near Southampton for a part-time role over the course of 2 months. It didn't really make economic sense but it made me light up inside and that was enough for now.

I felt like this was the gentle shove I needed. I was sick and fed up, and the feeling of not taking it petrified me.

So, I applied for the job and went for an interview. The company, Future Foundations were based in London. An extraordinary company dedicated to helping young people fulfil their life potential; offering soft skill development and education in some of the crucial areas of life that schools can't always focus on; like building self-awareness and confidence, teamwork and communication skills; and inspiring people to become leaders in our society. I was so on board and put everything into getting the job.

This place called London was pulling me closer. I had a calling to move.

I used to think London wasn't the kind of place I'd want to live or I could live. Like many northerners, I thought it was too busy, too expensive and too posh. But after living and working there the summer before, my mind was open to the multicultural magic of the place.

I took the leap of faith I needed.

I accepted the job with Future Foundations and didn't look back. I quit my part-time job at Tesco's and made plans to leave. It was one of the most phenomenal feelings of freedom I'd experienced. Whatever happened, I was free again. I felt alive. Like a huge weight was taken off my shoulders. I stood differently. I walked confidently. I ran home with sheer joy.

This is one of the moments I knew I was finding my way. I took an opportunity to do great work that was aligned with my passions and skillsets. I was taking a measured risk and I was doing what I truly wanted to do. Not following anyone else's hopes or wishes. I was living my own decision. It was measured bravery and promised to be lots of fun.

I had thirty days left in my current job. And whilst I was headed for a new opportunity, it was only a temporary contract so I needed a way to sustain myself in London.

The secret 'Designer in Disguise' project was still alive so I decided to finish what I started. Being motivated from a purposeful place, I did truly want to help Tesco and genuinely thought I could.

I focused on writing up my insights and wrote a letter to the CEO.

Two days later I received an email from the PA of the CEO. They invited me to meet the Head of UK Operations at their Head Office just outside of London. This was happening.

Whilst a few sceptics doubted my plan, I wasn't at all surprised. My level of conviction and certainty about speaking to the CEO was 100%.

This was going to be the big career breakthrough I needed. I thought I deserved it and I thought I was ready for it.

Secretly, I was desperate for this to be a fast route to being "successful". I thought, the more successful I am, the easier it will be for me to be honest about my struggles and insecurities. I was hiding something and I was afraid to let it show. Perhaps this could create a platform I could stand on? A position of authority that would give me the confidence I craved.

*

Then things happened really quickly. I approached my colleague, Louise, and together we prepared for the opportunity.

I had all, but one of my eggs in this basket. The other egg was in a world of learning and development, but I hadn't cracked it to know how it would turn out. So this was really important to me. I'd spent two years since graduating university in search of success of this kind.

We arrived at the office in Welwyn Garden City just outside of London. The first meeting was everything I wished it would be. I shared some insights and our approach to change was radically different to what they were focused on. I was in total flow and excited by the possibility of making change on this kind of scale. I really cared about people enjoying their work. I cared about systems being beautifully effective and nice to work with. I cared about managers helping people grow and develop. And I thought this was going to be the moment I'd realise all of those wishes.

After getting our message across, we were asked a simple question.

"So what do you want to do?" The Director asked us.

We'd enlightened them, surprised them and built enough credibility to propose working together. Little did they know I was effectively homeless in London and didn't really know what I was doing - I just got really annoyed and found some problems I wanted to solve.

We weren't a company and I wasn't a trained consultant. I hadn't studied business and I had no experience pitching for work of this kind, or at all. I essentially had a manufacturing degree, some big ideas and I was enthusiastic about changing things. I was a young man stuck inside the limiting label of a designer who really wanted to change the world.

Above all, I was a little bit all over the place emotionally. My suit and tie helped me hold it together for the meeting, but underneath I still felt lost.

Fortunately, the director didn't pressure us to come up with an answer there and then.

We had some time to put a proposal together and present the senior team with a plan.

From this point forward, there was no plan.

Chapter 7

# EPISODE TWO

Ego says, "Once everything falls into place, I'll
find peace". Spirit says, "Find your peace
and everything will fall into place".

- Marianne Williamson

It was all too familiar. I was anxious. I was scared. I couldn't bear the feelings I had. It was happening again. I dragged myself into a second serious episode of depression. Another nervous breakdown loomed over me. What I thought was a one-off production was about to have a sequel.

The catalyst for this episode was similar to the last - I clearly hadn't learnt my lesson. But this time I knew deep down what I needed to do. The answer was much clearer.

I'd taken the plunge. I was in London at last, but without a home. Regardless of what the following months would bring, I needed a solid foundation to begin building from; without a home, I knew I wouldn't last very long. I needed to find a place to live.

Luckily, I wasn't completely homeless. In the middle of my first week of work with Future Foundations, a colleague called Terence said I could stay with him while I figured things out.

He lived on a converted ship in Barking in the East of London - an outrageous and wonderful place to live. I remember telling my friends and family I was living on a fancy boat, they struggled to understand just as much as I did. I thought people lived in houses and flats, and people that went to sea lived on boats, but in London, apparently not.

The boat was a converted mining ship with sixteen bedrooms split into four apartments, each with a spacious living room and a shared outside space on the top deck. For the next two weeks, I made myself at home on the sofa, being careful not to let my patch of allocated space expand too far. It gave me a base for the remainder of the work contract with Future Foundations.

At this point, everything was fine. I was still in a short-term mindset. I was naive about what I was actually doing. I was on the verge of becoming fully independent for the first time in my life - not supported by student loans or university or my parents.

After I few weeks, the anxiety began again. The uncontrollable feelings inside of me kept rising to the surface. Even though I knew it was in my mind, I tried to pretend it was not there, but ignoring it didn't make it go away. Instead, it just festered and waited patiently to reemerge when the time was right.

I was starting to struggle. This time I was more open about it and I told Terence how I was feeling. We'd become close in the few weeks we'd known each other and I felt I could trust him. He was open, kind and the caring friend I needed. I told him how anxious

I was about making a permanent decision to live in London. My honesty gave me a bit more time but I knew this couldn't go on for much longer.

My struggle to commit to living in London did have a logical barrier. I didn't have much money saved and didn't have work lined up so didn't want to take a reckless risk until I was more confident I'd be able to support myself. I wanted a good start.

But beneath this logical argument came a surge of truth. My inability to make a confident decision came from my low self-esteem. Something inside of me was scared of the future. Scared that if I committed to something long-term, I'd open the door to seeking the truth within myself. Beneath my outward confidence to make things happen, was a very insecure young man, afraid of my own life ahead of me. Terrified more than I thought anyone would understand.

Most housing contracts are six or twelve months. I wanted to take one week at a time, the thought of being in one place for a long time frightened me. I thought, the sooner I find my own place and make a home, the sooner I'll have to face what's really going on.

I took some time away to clear my head. Thankfully, I had some other friends living in London too. I spent a few days hunting for job opportunities and the evenings enjoying their company to keep sanity levels topped up.

After a couple of weeks, I had overstayed their generous hospitality; I moved on again – this time to living in hostels. I needed to be away from anybody that might ask me what I was doing. I didn't really know and I didn't want to talk about it.

I dotted around the area of London I was most familiar with, a place called Elephant and Castle. I'd stayed there once before on a University trip. While sleeping in close proximity to up to thirty other people wasn't ideal, it was what I needed at the time. Hostel living as a traveller exploring the world is money well spent. But it somehow doesn't have the same appeal in your own country. The casual vibe, slight messiness and the overly-friendly nature of people was sometimes just too much. I told a few people what I was up to but I mostly did my own thing.

It was a pretty lonely time. Two nights was the most I stayed in one place and then I moved on to another hostel.

\*

After some time away and spending my money slowly and tactfully, I knew I had to commit. And as if luck would have it, a room was available to live on the converted boat with my friend Terence. And as a newcomer to the city, I'd have a good group of people to begin my adventure with. It was within my budget and it was available immediately.

But the vibe wasn't quite right. It was a world away from what I was used to and I wasn't comfortable living there. I wanted to be in the city where the magic was happening. I know beggars can't be choosers, but it wasn't right. So – "Andy, learn your lesson from Chapter 1 – let go. Walk away and find somewhere that is right for you. Stop feeling the need to please other people. Find some conviction. Be honest. Be brave. Be yourself."

I didn't. I was so tired of this whole house hunting, job searching, thinking process, that I thought I should just live there. I was so grateful to my friend for giving me a place to live that I thought I owed it to him to stay there. So I recklessly tried to convince myself I needed to commit to living there. I thought this was the barrier I needed to push through.

I remember calling my auntie to ask her opinion. Since my experience with depression, I knew that I probably wasn't in the best frame of mind to make a rational decision, so I asked for help. I called my auntie as we'd become quite close since my I'd opened up about my mental health struggles. She was very understanding and she had experience working in mental health so she could empathise with what I was going through.

I wanted her to decide for me. My auntie being a very grounded, wise and wonderful human being told me exactly what to do.

"You need to trust yourself. Do whatever you need to do for you. No one else can make a true decision for you. I am here for you, but I can't decide for you."

I felt trapped again, between doing something and doing the right thing. I was scared and panicking.

I took a taxi half away across London to move a step closer. The vacant room was open. I could secretly spend the night there and make the payments the following day. That's what I did. The taxi journey was like the eye of the storm. A little moment of peace that was out of my control. When I got out in Barking, it was decision time.

Knowing I didn't want to be there, I lay in bed like a ball of anxiety. I thought back to how I felt a week earlier sitting in Leicester Square. On a little adventure to clear my head, I stopped and sat on the pavement with my back to the cold stone wall. I looked up at the bright lights as if to find some inspiration. I would hate my mum to know how I was feeling and what I was going through. I wondered if anyone could understand. This self-inflicted emotional misery I was putting myself through was too painful and I prayed it would get better.

I looked up at the lights and thought about the song that my mum played for me a year earlier. "I can be astonishing...I can be astonishing"...the lyrics gave me a little glimpse of hope that it would somehow be okay. I thought about other people that could have been in a similar situation, feeling their life was about something more. People longing to know what it was all about, and a believing it could all be what they dreamt it could be.

That moment in Leicester Square was one of those in-between moments. A place I needed to push through in order to reach the place I wanted to be.

*

I lay in bed looking up at the ceiling. It was an odd shaped room, as you would expect from a ship. It had a raised double bed and a really cool desk suspended from the ceiling. The window was small which made it a little claustrophobic. There were so many cool features I liked. But I couldn't enjoy it.

My stomach was churning. I didn't unpack because I knew I wasn't staying. I knew I had to get out. I knew what I had to do. I had to acknowledge what my insecurity was and where it was coming from.

The silence made me truly feel and truly listen to my fear for the first time.

I was scared of questioning my sexuality.

For at least a few years, I'd had this swirling of doubt inside me. A doubt that had festered and grown. A doubt that I'd managed to suppress for a long time. I channelled all of my energy at university into my studies. And all of my energy since then into finding the perfect career. I really thought having success in my career would give me the confidence to look at myself and be who I truly was. I thought, "I'm going to wait until I make loads of money, or do something really special before I discover who I am."

My mind raced forward. I started to realise that committing to signing a house would also mean being open to being in a relationship. I couldn't use the excuse any longer that I didn't want to meet anyone because I want a long term relationship because I was moving away. I'd moved and here I was. I'd pushed myself so close to a decision I didn't want to make, that it forced me to be real with what was actually stopping me.

I was scared I might be gay.

I didn't know how to process my feelings. All of my fears flooded through me. I didn't know how my life would unfold. I didn't know what it meant to live a gay lifestyle. I didn't know how I'd be a parent. I didn't know what my friends would think. I didn't know if I'd be the same person. I felt so much shame and so much confusion.

The feeling of admitting this to myself and to other people was horrifying.

All the years of my childhood and adolescence, I'd heard people using derogatory terms of homosexual abuse, often as throw away comments without much conscious thought. "Stop being such a poof. You stupid fag. Stop being gay about it. Do it, you bender." And so on. The negative and emasculating associations with being gay, made it feel like a cowardly thing to be. I wanted to be strong.

I wanted to be what I thought a typical man was. I wanted to be liked and loved and happy.

But enough was enough, I had to tell someone.

I told the closest person to me. Someone I knew loved me and always would. I called my Mum.

It was a huge barrier to my life and happiness, I had to let it out. It cast too much doubt over my future that I couldn't be certain about anything. It coloured so many decisions I made and it was about to culminate and overflow again.

I needed to tell just one person. I needed to say it out loud.

My heart beat faster and faster. I hadn't slept the night before. I was tired and confused. A panic attack was building. I didn't want another panic attack. I knew how scary they were, there was only one way I could get out of it.

I'd decided to tell my Mum I thought I was gay. I knew it would be fine. She's lovely and wonderful, I had no doubt she'd support me.

Locked in my room, I held the phone in my hand and pressed call. My body flooded with nerves. I could barely breathe.

"Mum. I need to talk to you and tell you something that's really going to be hard for me. It's caused me so much pain for so long. I just need to tell someone".

My aim was to allude to what I was talking about without actually saying it. But my Mum being a great listener, did exactly that.

"It's okay. Whatever it is, we love you. Just tell me".

"Okay…". I took a deep breath. And another. I focused on breathing to stop the panic. I felt like I was going to be sick. I simultaneously blurted out and cried…"Mum, I think I might be gay".

I continued to cry and waited for my Mum to respond. I wasn't sure what I wanted. I couldn't really think. I wanted acceptance, but I wasn't sure why I was crying so much. Maybe to acknowledge I was ashamed? As if to mirror the views of people that thought it wasn't the right thing to be.

My Mum responded exactly as I knew she would, with love and no judgment. She reassured me that it was okay and she was grateful that I had the courage to tell her.

I was confused and scared, but I'd said it. "I am gay."

Now could I be happy?

It was out. It was all over. Or at least I hoped it would be.

I'd given attention to a deep seeded secret about myself. Years of anxiety bubbling under the surface. Years of not being confident in who I was. And years of not feeling enough.

But nothing actually changed within me. I still felt sort of the same. I was still Andy. But I did feel a sense a freedom I hadn't felt in a very long time.

For the first time, I was able to actually breathe and be content with the courage I had shown. However my life played out, this was a massive accomplishment. I was able to be so honest and vulnerable in front of my Mum.

For now, I had my conviction back.

Chapter 8

# PEACE IN THE PANIC

"Good order is the foundation of all things"

- Edmund Burke

The next morning I decided the boat life wasn't for me. I picked up my bags that I hadn't unpacked and headed to a new hostel. I needed to be on my own and allow the craziness to subside. I told the landlord I wasn't going to live there. I said I was struggling with depression, using it as leverage to make him sympathise with my irrational behaviour. He kindly agreed to back my deposit.

Off I trundled back to Elephant and Castle. It perhaps wasn't the nicest part of London to be in, but it was familiar. I didn't want to think anymore.

*

Jumping into new opportunities that we feel excited by is a very exciting way to live life. Our hearts and instincts can take us on wonderful adventures if we are willing to put some of the over-thinking and analysis on hold. Three of my favourite leaps of faith took me to San Francisco for a conference that changed my career plans, to Camp America that made me see the possibilities of outdoor education and to a conference about money, that taught me what I didn't know I needed to learn.

There were times on my journey when a little bit of practicality would have saved me a lot of heartaches. Being overly optimistic is sometimes beautiful and sometimes hard to take.

My bold plunge to chase an opportunity in London left me stranded and dependent on others. I had no financial security and no savings, just a tunnel vision, gung-ho, all in mentality and an obsession with believing it would all work out. And you could say it did, I survived, but I didn't enjoy my quality of life for a long time and I don't wish to do it again.

I learnt that there are times to run towards opportunities and there are times we need to be a little bit more calculated. While I can look back and take strength from surviving and building a great life, for enduring time spent on sofa's and living in hostels, for dragging all my possessions around London in desperation – I learnt the hard way what it means to be responsible for yourself.

\*

I rested for a couple of days and then looked for short term letting options. I had to find somewhere to live semi-permanently if I was going to succeed in establishing my life in London.

I had the second Tesco meeting coming up and the promise of freelance work in the new year, but before I could give any real thought and attention to that, I had to get my living situation in order.

I found a room in a shared house. I had no idea how competitive this world of room letting was. Because London is such a saturated market, anyone with a room to let can invite anywhere between five and ten people to look around, until they find the person that will best suit their house. Someone that is fun enough, but not too wild and someone tidy, but not a clean freak. But most importantly, you must be able to get on with the people in the house and fit into their way of living.

On this occasion, my Geordie nature was enough to give me the edge. I was moving in with four others, none were from the UK: a Kiwi, an Aussie, a South African and an Italian. A beautiful cultural mix and a fair representation of Clapham, the area of South London I was would be living in.

I finally had my own room for longer than a few days. If by exposing and sharing a personal truth, I had a sense of freedom within myself, I had now a freedom of movement too. I could cook my own food. I could come and go without needing to alert anyone.

I had a month or two to get it all together, both emotionally and financially.

*

It was now nearly Christmas, so my timing wasn't great in terms of things happening in a work context. But I'd managed to extend my stay in the house for another month, as one of the guys was going travelling.

I headed home for a few days to see my family for Christmas and returned for a New Year party in London. Coincidently, the party was in Elephant and Castle, my hostel hopping stomping ground. But I was beginning to see London in a whole new light. After all of the madness I'd pushed myself through, I had a big glimmer of light in the sky.

I stood on a roof terrace overlooking the London skyline watching the New Year firework display. I hoped it was going to be a happy new year. I was making new friends and I was starting to see how life could be in London.

*

Getting it together financially was a case of being proactive and pursuing work opportunities, along with being conservative with spending and resourceful with my budget. But getting it together emotionally was more important, if I was cool, calm and collected in my thoughts and attitude, I'd have a much better chance of getting to where I wanted to be.

I had a plan. I decided to take up yoga. I did a quick Google search and found a place nearby. It was close enough to home so I wouldn't spend any money travelling and they offered daily classes that would give some structure and purpose to my days.

This would be my third attempt at yoga. More and more people kept telling me about the benefits it brought to them and I was more ready than ever to receive the benefits myself.

My first yoga experience I wasn't so ready. I took a class when I was at University with a few of the guys I lived and studied with. We all walked in with naive arrogance and sat at the back, both to show we were beginners and to not seem overly keen for this slightly strange practice. We were open-minded enough to give it a go, but not enough to take it seriously. The physical challenge shocked us and left us aching for days. The spiritual aspect moved us closer to laughter than any form of deeper connection with ourselves. We laughed and joked at the back of the class and let our immaturity keep our egos safe.

My second experience was a lot more committed. I took to the mat for a second time in my depression recovery days living in Newcastle. With a few more years of maturity on my side and a few months working with an older colleague who practiced regularly, it was the perfect motivation to try again. I went to the class confident about doing it, but little did I know it would be twenty-nine middle-aged women, and me.
"It shouldn't matter that I'm the only guy…" I thought to myself. "You are here for the yoga, not to make friends or be approved or be judged. Just do the yoga".

I did do the yoga and I really enjoyed it and thanked the teacher for her support with my introduction to the beginners class. But I struggled to say I would come back and I think she could sense my unease with being the only guy. I really liked the class, I just wasn't confident enough in myself to block out all of the judgment. The judgment coming from me thinking that for some reason they'd be judging me. I knew it benefitted me greatly but I overthought the whole thing. At the end of the class, she told me that she trained the Newcastle United Football Team. I thought "aha, this is a thing for guys!" A good boost for my masculine ego, but not enough to make me get a membership. My ego guard dog wanted to protect me and sadly pressed pause on my yoga.

Now fast forward to London, I was again more open minded. After lots of emotional breakthroughs and much more confidence in myself, coupled with living in a city that was extremely open minded to all of this yoga activity, my hand was forced.

As I sat in my room, trying to stay warm in the cold Winter days, I searched online for nearby Yoga classes. My room was in the attic and badly insulated, the windows were single glazed so I covered them with towels to keep some heat in. It wasn't a very well looked after house and my ice cold feet were paying the price.
I found a local studio that did hot yoga. I didn't really need to read the description about what "hot yoga" actually meant. All I knew was that I wanted to do yoga and I wanted to be warm, hot would be a bonus. I signed up and went for a trial class. In every challenging moment, I thought about the frost forming on my windows at home. I was happy there.

For thirty days straight I attended yoga, making the most of my thirty-day trial membership. Without an actual job or anything to do, I had something to get up for. A place that was warm and a practice that I knew was beneficial for my mental and emotional wellbeing. In all of the mania of my life decisions, life uncertainty, and life distress – I found a way to slow down.

This title of this chapter 'peace in the panic' describes how I was able to feel in these moments. I had so much I could choose to worry about. And so much that wasn't as I wanted it to be. But if I felt good within myself, I exercised and I had a mindfulness practice I had every chance of making things work.

Chapter 9

# A MIRACLE

"Your need for acceptance can
make you invisible in this world".

- Jim Carey

It was the big day I'd been waiting for. It was time to pitch to Tesco.

All of the clever visualisation exercises, helped me believe I would get this meeting, but I lacked clarity in where I wanted my work and career to go. I wasn't really confident in anything I was doing. I got the recognition I craved but was lost on what to do next.

I decided to enlist the support of two other people, which only made things worse. Another designer friend called Caspar and a more experienced consultant called James. I was doing what I thought was right, but equally blowing the opportunity way out of proportion. ON reflection, forcing something that wasn't meant to be. I had more voices to listen to, more ideas to take on board and more reasons to doubt the conviction of my own inner voice.

Things started to spiral out of control. I started to expose my anxiety. All of the leadership ability I thought I had started to fade away.

My unsettled life in London and my unsettled mind made it all very hard work. I began to lose my vision of what I thought I wanted. I was in dire need of paid work because I needed the money to live. I was desperate.

We all had ideas. It was like mixing paint with too many colours and ending up with a dark mess. This was a big realisation; I couldn't possibly lead until I could learn how to live. Once I was in place of happiness, contentment, and purpose, I'd have a foundation to lead from. Right now, I just wanted this journey to end so I could focus on myself and get my life in order.

I wanted to quit, walk away and cry into a corner.

With a few weeks to prepare, we did the best we could. After several meetings, we had drafted and re-drafted a proposal, getting ready to pitch again to a larger team.

As the day got closer my usual optimism started to fade.

I felt that something wasn't right. This wasn't what I truly wanted. This wasn't how things were supposed to go. Perhaps I needed to come all of this way to find what I was really looking for. And perhaps I would one day consult with Tesco. But there was no way I was going to do this now. If I seemed together on the surface, underneath I was cracking like a window.

I felt like I'd beaten myself.

We showed up to the second meeting ready to perform. One voice in my head was championing me to succeed, with seven others telling me it was over. I prepared myself to give it everything we had, just on the off chance it came off; it would be an opportunity that could be very lucrative and a great learning experience.

As a young and fairly inexperienced team, we challenged the senior leadership team and presented in a way they didn't expect. We left the clichéd PowerPoint's at home and showed up to engage in our own style. And even with their experienced risk adverse hats on, something was beginning to turn in our favour.

I thought, "perhaps the negativity was just in my mind, after all, maybe we could still do this".

We knew the opportunity alone was a form of success, but without a contract, I didn't have much to live in London with. So we pushed, persuaded and prodded them towards a big committed decision to work with us. And for most of the meeting, it looked like they were going to find a way.

We got so close. I desperately wanted this story to escalate into how I became successful at such a young age. How I managed to create a business opportunity with one of the UK's biggest companies. How I was so amazing.
But that wasn't going to be the case.
Now wasn't the right time for Tesco to work with us and now wasn't the right time for me to be pursuing this kind of work. While I knew we could have done more to push them over the line of fear

and into the "let's risk it" mindset, it wasn't to be. In truth, I'd already accepted personal defeat and I knew I was climbing the wrong ladder to find happiness.

If I thought getting a huge complex work opportunity could bring me happiness, I would have been very wrong. Failure was a gift in disguise.

The moment we heard the decision that our proposal wouldn't be accepted, gave me a huge sense of relief. I was so exhausted. The emotional rollercoaster I was on was thankfully at an end. Even if a struggling financial situation was ahead of me, I knew I was lucky to escape this path.

I needed to get my things together first.

When I created the opportunity to speak to the directors of Tesco about a consulting opportunity, there was part of me that was so excited that it might actually happen. My underlying motivation was to help and to be of service, but unfortunately, the challenging emotional space I was in, made the leadership challenge I was about to face almost impossible. But in the face of failure, came a beautiful gift.

I had thought this was the kind of success I wanted. This was what I wanted to be proud of and talk about. But as I got to the door of the opportunity, I had a realisation. This isn't what I want to do and this isn't what's really important to me right now.

Not only did my naivety and inexperience make me mistake what I thought I wanted from what I actually wanted (which was a hugely valuable lesson in itself) but more importantly, the rejection gave me the freedom to do what I really needed to do.

What some people might have expected to be a demoralising day, was in fact liberating and freeing. I was immensely grateful that we didn't get the work, this helpful failure meant I could focus on the important work in my life.

I was gifted the freedom, to put myself first. I could stop pretending that outside achievement could gloss over my feeling of inadequacy inside. I needed to get myself into a happier and emotionally good place before I pursued entrepreneurial dreams.

I learnt that the important work I had to do was within myself.

Chapter 10

# RESPONSIBILITY

"If it's never our fault, we can't take personal
responsibility for it. If we can't take responsibility f
or it, we'll always be victim"

- Richard Bach


The time had come to pack up my bags again and wave goodbye
to my temporary home. My money was running out and I knew I
couldn't afford another month's rent.

Thankfully, I had two Geordie friends in London that I'd met at
University and they kindly offered me a place to stay. I was without
a home to call my own, but I didn't end up completely homeless.

They didn't have a spare room, so it was back to the sofa, or in this
case a delightfully comfy airbed. Every evening I inflated it and
every morning I let it down to re-order the flat. I tried to be as
considerate as possible to avoid my suitcase belongings spilling into
their lives. My rent contribution was buying them a nice new
cooking pot, I thought the gesture felt more valuable than the
money value alone. On top of that, I cooked whenever they were
there and attempted to be as helpful as possible. I tried to make it
almost better that I was there, opposed to it feeling like an
inconvenience.

I was hugely grateful they offered a place that allowed me to keep my head above the water. I was at a crucial time in cementing my life in London. I had a little bit of future freelance facilitation work, but not enough to risk signing for a house.

I used the remaining money I had left on food and living as minimally as I possibly could. I had to find work quickly and I had to let go of my grand entrepreneurial dreams temporarily.

*

One of my toughest decisions came as I looked at my depleting funds. I was applying for work and being proactive to create income but in the meantime I needed money. I had a choice to make, do I reach out to my parents and ask to borrow some money or do I embrace humility and claim government benefits?

I was pretty much unemployed. I only had the promise of future freelance income ahead of me, nothing guaranteed.

It wasn't an easy decision. On the one hand, I wanted to keep building my reputation of doing creative freelance consultancy work. I feared that if people knew I claimed benefits, their opinion of me would change. On top of that, I wasn't sure how to think about myself as being unemployed and claiming benefits. I'd have to go to the job centre and fully acknowledge I'd messed up. I'd have to surrender to needing financial help.
I'd taken a big risk, it didn't pay off and I had to sort it out.

Another option was to borrow money from my family. I knew they had faith in me that I'd figure things out, so borrowing some money would have been okay. It would have just been until I found more work.

As I talked myself into this plan, I knew what I had to do. It was up to me to do this. I couldn't avoid it any longer. I couldn't pretend everything was going to be okay. It wouldn't be unless I made it so.

Our UK Government support system is there to help people who need it. I'd paid tax towards the system and I knew I was entitled to get some support.

I felt pretty low. I had lots of qualifications and a first class degree. I came from an amazing background and supportive family. I'd been employed and I'd just decided I needed to leave of my own accord.

I got ready to go to the Job Centre.

I took the bus from Brixton to Clapham Old Town and walked with a little conviction, as if to hide the shame I felt. I looked up at the old building, trying desperately to separate what I was thinking about myself and instead focus on what I needed to do. I just needed a little bit of money to keep me going.

I sat amongst people that were clearly in very different situations to myself. Some people were fairly presentable, but others were a little less so. Clothing aside, though, as soon as I set foot in the building,

I felt a wave of energy being zapped from my body. People seemed to just be drifting through the motions - both employees and job seekers alike. I felt like I was being coated in apathy. The atmosphere was draining and lifeless. "How did I end up here?"

I filled out the necessary paperwork and sat in line for an appointment. I wanted to be in and out. I've never been fond of overly complex bureaucratic systems, but I knew I had to be patient. I knew I couldn't change the system I was about to be processed through.

As I sat amongst the other jobless candidates, I started to guess what their stories might be. What led them to be seeking income support? Where did they come from and how did they end up here? Were they regulars or first timers? Did they feel hopeful or hopeless?

I tried to stop myself being judgemental. Part of me thought I didn't need to be here. Part of me felt I didn't belong here. And part of me just went through the motions. Fighting the truth of my reality wasn't going to make it any better.

I left with an action plan of jobs to apply for and three weekly goals to meet before I'd receive any money. I walked out with a slower walk to get the bus and headed back to my friends' flat. I sat looking out of the window with a feeling of regretful accomplishment. I regretted the fact I'd put myself in this situation, but I was proud I'd managed to be responsible and take this step.

I waited for Jonny and Max to come home from work to give me some company and take my mind off the stress I felt.

Little did I know, not having a registered home address was a real barrier to not getting income support. I left believing I might get some money, but in the end, the complex bureaucratic system meant I wouldn't be get anything until I had somewhere to live. A predicament I struggled with because I kind of needed the money to pay for somewhere to live.

*

As for getting a job, I didn't just want to just do any old thing. I was too proud and I thought I deserved more. Even if it was temporary work I couldn't bare the thought of going back to a lower skilled job. I needed something in line with where I wanted my career to take me. I wanted to be challenged. I wanted to be part of a purposeful organisation and I wanted to keep developing.

The perfect job opportunity arose. As if by magic, I was introduced to another youth organisation called MyBnk, they offered business and finance education to young people. The business programmes were short entrepreneurial projects that gave students an experience of actually running a real-life enterprise. The job role was to be an education officer to run the finance and enterprise programmes.

The training side of the job really instantly excited me. I knew it was the field of work I could excel in and the creative possibilities that entrepreneurship presented was very exciting. I'd spent the previous two years dipping my toes into the business world, so this was a delightful coincidence. The recommendation I had was from someone that used to work there, I was sold on it being a good fit.

But the more I thought about it, the full-time position gave me the feeling of being trapped. The creative side of me loved variety. I liked the idea in principle of having stable income and I'd never had a full-time job. It would give me the chance to get my finances together and find a place to live. The structure and consistency would also give me time outside of work to progress with my personal journey.

I was torn. I didn't want to give up the flexibility that self-employment allowed. I told myself it was the right thing to do, even though it didn't feel it was quite right. Once again, my intuition was saying one thing and my mind was saying another.

I applied for the role and gave it my best shot.

The interview was a practical training presentation combined with a panel interview. I felt such a good fit with the company, but I was frightened by the idea of being fully employed. I thought I might get comfortable and never leave to do my own thing. The interview was going well. My head nodded and smiled as if to affirm I want the job, but a little voice inside of me kept asking the challenging question. "Do you really want this? What are you doing? Are you sure?"
I got what I wanted.

They decided that based on my experience running innovation events, working for young enterprise and being generally passionate about business, I'd be better suited to being an enterprise trainer. And the best way for me to do that would be in a freelance position. They hired me as the first business freelancer in the company. Somehow they knew what I wanted better than I did. I got a job that wasn't advertised, a wonderful win/win situation! It gave me the financial security I needed, along with the flexible agenda I wanted.

I was now part of two companies and felt in a much better position to commit to living here in London.
I had no more excuses to hide from. My life moved up another level.

People say there are those moments in your life when you cross a bridge and know your life will never be the same. This was one of those moments.

# Chapter 11

# IT'S TIME

"Commitment is that turning point in your life
when you seize the moment and convert an
opportunity to alter your destiny"

- Immanuel Kant

Spring was edging closer and I felt much better about this transitional phase. I was determined to make this life in London a success. I had almost enough work through a few different sources to give me a stable monthly income, but I didn't feel fully in control. I had these grand dreams inside of me waiting to be shared with the world but I was still living on a sofa and something was missing inside.

As my priority had never been to earn and save money, I hadn't earned very much and I certainly hadn't saved any. My living circumstances directly reflected what I thought about money - it wasn't important and I didn't need very much. The sofa and minimal belongings were enough to represent how little attention I gave gaining more.

In the short term, I needed money to create stability in my life. I wanted freedom, like a living ship that could sail freely from island to island. And in the longer term I wanted to pursue my own projects, so for both to happen I needed to go to the school of personal finance.

*

As if by chance the universe and a friend conspired to help me learn what I needed to learn. The week after acknowledging my financial pressure, I was given a free ticket to a money management seminar. As I was starting to train and coach in the field of personal development, I was being opened up to events designed to give people the support they needed.

Had I been given his invitation a few year or even months earlier, I would never have taken it. It was an American self-help seminar called "Millionaire Mind-set Intensive". Being a millionaire was not on my radar at all.

My life on the outside looked and felt pretty desperate. There weren't many things I would have said no to, to improve my situation - especially not a free ticket to a seminar that could help me with my financial troubles. It was a personal challenge that was keeping me house hopping, with nowhere to call home. Believing money wasn't important made me very poor.

Thankfully I didn't overthink the opportunity, I knew it would help me begin to resolve some of the hang-ups I had about money. And hopefully give me some skills to manage my money better - an independent lifestyle in one of the most expensive cities in the world requires you to have your things together when it comes to money.

I arrived on a Friday morning at 9 am ready for an elaborate and intensive three-day experience. As I entered the space, it was very reminiscent of the culture of American summer camp. Extremely high energy, overtly friendly people and it felt like a genuinely inspiring space.

I walked in being the money sceptic thinking "it's not about the money... I don't care about it...I just want to do good work...money is for greedy people...it changes people. Why are people so obsessed with it?"

I always thought that as a creative person, being overly concerned about money would stifle my creativity. And that somehow you couldn't have money and do good work. I thought I was so intrinsically motivated to do meaningful work, I didn't need to care about money. That it was somehow an evil troublemaker that caused problems for people.

It was a stream of consciousness that I'd never realised I'd had before. I'd created so much attachment and negative associations with money; it was so emotive and powerful that it had so much control over my life in ways I hadn't considered. I'd always resisted conversations about money, talking about it made my stomach swirl and gave me an uncomfortable feeling. I knew this was something I needed to change.

Once again, it was meeting like-minded people that made my journey so much easier. People that believed what I did, cared about what I did and understood where I'd been, where I was and where I wanted to go. I got the chance to work through some hard emotional past experiences that were affecting me and I got to try a lot of NLP (Neuro Linguistic Programming) techniques. This whole world of seminars was intriguing and very new to me. But as free weekend experiences go, I was hugely grateful for the opportunity.

This was somehow part of the learning I needed on my journey, and it wasn't just about money. This was an opportunity to learn about how my life on the outside was shaped by what I believed on the inside. The seminar itself involved a lot of interactive exercises, some very informative education around financial management, but most importantly, several opportunities to explore my own relationship with money.

Even though I wasn't financially any better off, I knew how to control one important aspect of my life. All of the new techniques, strategies and attitudes I would have to apply and ingrain into my life.

*

Sunday evening I left inspired and totally exhausted. After three, twelve-hour days, I coasted home back to my friend's sofa. A different friend again, probably the last person I could call upon to help me out.

The following week came quickly, it was time to leave my friend's place and wave goodbye to another sofa and temporary home. I was going to miss their company, but I'd used up their generous hospitality. I moved into a nice shared house about three miles up the road in Clapham South.

I felt like I was sort of progressing and my life was moving forward. It certainly wasn't boring and static. But I knew this short-term letting couldn't carry on forever. Unpacking and repacking was driving me into the ground. I felt unsettled again and I was sick of suitcase living; a few things in the wardrobe and tiptoeing around a house that wasn't really mine, trying to abide by their unwritten rules. Perhaps I was being a little ungrateful and not appreciating what I had and maybe I was getting ahead of myself thinking I deserved a better quality of living. But the truth was, I felt alone and I was desperate for some consistency, a place to be and be able to build a life from.

For the month of March, I embraced things as much as I could. My highlight of the month was a day of activities on Clapham Common, a lovely big park in South London that was right next to my house. With a group of colleagues, that quickly became my close friends, we played rounders, football and other fun games. Our highlight being egg catching; where you take turns throwing an egg to your partner and after each throw, you step further and further apart – ending up throwing it as far as you can and inevitably it breaks on one of you.

These times of fun gave me hope that life could be fun. In between the emotional journey I'd been on, there was perhaps light at the end of the tunnel and good times ahead. It made me stop fighting and forcing my situation too much and helped me see that my life here could be amazing. Once I stopped fighting with myself and started to live a little, happiness was closer than I realised. This was another moment I look back and think this is another example of living on purpose. Despite a lot of my life not being in full flowing order, I managed to create a window of bliss and allow myself to freely enjoy life as it was.

And later that week, another door of opportunity opened. Two of my colleagues at Future Foundations, James, and Kate, were looking to move into a new house. Kate worked in the office team and James had been away travelling, so I didn't really know them at all. But the kind of company we worked for, helping young people and being lovers of exciting education, said a lot about our common values.

In principle, this was a very straight forward decision. Our values were very aligned and we were of a similar age and in very similar situations. We all wanted somewhere to call home.

As I quickly said yes to the invitation, a little voice in my head took my attention. The fizzling's of doubt started to swirl and the significance of moving into a permanent place made me second guess myself, again.
"Am I ready for this? I don't even know these two people… They work for the same company, so they are probably really nice. But

what if things don't work out? What if I can't be myself? What if it forces me to…."

I stopped the negative train of thought and shook my head to regain a positive focus. If I didn't do this now, when was I going to do it? The thought of temporary living frightened me more than making this commitment. And thankfully I went through with it. This is the part of the story that starts to turns more positive and away from the destructive personal path I was on.

April 4th, 2013, we moved in. James and I collected the keys and started moving our things in; Kate was away on holiday so joined us a week later.

Once we signed and moved in, I was met by a combination of delightful feelings. Relief that I knew I had twelve months to be in one place, excitement that I had new housemates to get to know and renewed confidence in myself. I did this despite being afraid.

The three of us had a beer and a picnic in a nearby park to celebrate after work. We got to know each other a little bit and drew straws to help decide who would get each room. There were two bigger rooms and one smaller one. Kate had more stuff and she really didn't want the smaller room, but she still agreed straws were the fairest system. And to Kate's delight, she got the biggest room and I got the smallest. But in the grand scheme of things, this wasn't really important.

After six months of temporary living, home hoping and intruding on other people's spaces – I had a home to call my own.

Whilst people may read this and think, you just moved into a house. It wasn't the moving that was the significant bit. It was what it represented. With time I could figure this out and start to understand how to move beyond the internal things that were holding me back from true happiness.

Chapter 12

# LOVING TO LIVE

"Rules for happiness: something to do,
someone to love, something to hope for"

- Emmanuel Kent

May came around very quickly as we all enjoyed our first few months of our new house. We lived near a huge park, very close to a delicious Italian ice cream shop and relatively close to the city. It was all still new, but a much more familiar environment. The three of us had lots of fun living together and making our house a home.

Life was good on the work front. I had training contracts lined up and a few freelance jobs too, and I had a home at last. When I set off from Newcastle to London, it wasn't the journey I'd expected or the six months I had planned. The scary roller-coaster had at least stopped for a while and let me catch my breath.

A few weeks went by and the excitement of moving in had worn off. Sitting in my room, all alone, I thought the time ahead would be challenging. I knew a lot of the emotional pain I was feeling, wouldn't just disappear.

I thought ahead to the coming months of my life, imagining myself on a long runway. I wanted to be at the other end, on the other side of this journey. I wanted a helicopter to help me escape. I'd be able to fly high and spin around so people could look up to me and think – you are special, you are cool and you are wonderful. I didn't want to feel my way through any more difficult thoughts or push beyond any more pain I felt. I just wanted it all to be over.

I closed my eyes and thought about racing towards my career aspirations, as if that would somehow give me the sense of completion I was looking for. I knew enough, to know it wouldn't.

Without knowing what was really at the end of this imaginary runway, I continued my inward journey. I read more books, watched more TED talks and spent a lot of time in my room thinking about how I could change things for myself. Asking myself a simple but very important question - could I be happy? And I mean actually happy, not temporarily joyful because of a fun activity. But happy because I loved life and I loved myself.

Over the previous few years, I'd watched lots of great videos by Anthony Robbins, the American motivational speaker and life coach. I'd heard great things about his events and decided to attend one. Even though I was in a much more positive space, I still knew some unresolved things were keeping me at arm's length from happiness. Life was getting good. But I was on a roll with learning about myself and I wanted to keep going.

A few weeks later I was sitting alongside eight thousand people in a seminar called 'Unleash The Power Within'. The title sounded bold and very American. Part of me felt there was something within I was scared to unleash and the other part of me, felt there was a lot I was without. Either way, I had a lot of admiration for his work and hoped he could help me. I managed to get a ticket for a reasonable price.

At my lowest points, I craved being around supportive people. The events attracted me because they offered an inspiring space, away from the depressive mood of my bedroom. I knew I'd meet interesting people and I knew I'd feel motivated to achieve more from life.

At most of these events, there is a breakthrough experience of some kind, this one was fire walking. The activities are used as metaphors, to help people push through emotional and mental barriers. Almost every self-help author, spiritual teacher and life coach generally agree on this notion; master your mind - be in control of your thoughts – be in control of your life.

On the first evening of the seminar, I was about to walk across burning hot coals. Whenever I have to take my socks and shoes off for an activity, it's usually fun and this was no exception. We learnt the psychology, we entered a hypnotic state, we got our psyche in the right state and all eight thousand of us marched outside to experience it together. Even though it felt like a military operation, all I could focus on was whether I'd actually be able to do it. Could I walk across burning hot coals? I would soon find out.

The energy was emphatic and the experience was really powerful. I marched across, as instructed and successfully walked across burning hot coals. It was quite surreal and it was over so quickly.

But as impressive as it sounds, the adrenaline passed and I got back to why I was there. I was sat in my seat thinking about what I truthfully wanted to get from the experience.

At the Millionaire Mind event the month earlier, we ended with a similar breakthrough exercise – except that time I was snapping an arrow on my neck. It was a safely organised process and a powerful message; even if you think you can't do something, you probably just need to push through the fear.

To give the exercise personal meaning, we had to link the event to something we wanted to work on, something that was holding us back. I wrote on the arrow "self-acceptance and sexuality". It was like poisonous secret still lurking inside of me. Nobody else in the group knew what I wrote and it didn't matter - they had their own things to work on, this was one of mine.

I put my socks and shoes back on, taking a moment to reflect on what I'd just done: walk across fire. For some people, it may have been their pinnacle moment, but that wasn't why I was there. Deep down it was my lack of confidence in who I was that was really holding me back. Not visible on the surface and never really spoken about, but deep down the feelings were so intense and scared me to think about. My breakthrough came in a very straightforward exercise with one key question.

Late that evening, we did an exercise to self-assess our levels of happiness or fulfilment in different areas of life. Rating our work, finances, physical bodies and emotional wellbeing. We gave them all a mark out of ten, I rated all of them around five or six, everything was okay – expect one category. In the relationship section, Tony Robbins told me to put zero. He said it with such conviction.

A sinking feeling rushed through me. My eyes closed to help me process the intense feeling. It was the first time I'd been asked to question why I wasn't in a relationship and why I hadn't been in one since I was at University. I started to think about the significance of neglecting this area of my life, thinking about what was stopping me seeing the value of romance and an intimate relationship.

"Wherever you have a low score - this is where you need to pay attention".

I was beginning to realise this is why I was really here. I could learn to be healthier and have more energy, I could remove mental blocks and earn more money and I could learn to overcome fears that were stopping me taking risks. All of the aims of living a more successful life were trying to steal my attention. Like little voices competing to show their importance. When was I going to be able to change that number from a zero? When was I going to be able to be in a relationship?

When I started writing this book I wanted to avoid the topic of relationships. I thought this book is going to just be about me and what I have discovered through my own journey to Living on Purpose. But as we get towards the truth of this topic, it's inevitable I needed to be honest about my experience of relationships.

I was right in the heart of exploring the inner puzzle of life and happiness, we are social beings by nature, destined to have relationships as a part of our lives. As friends, family, colleagues and loved ones. I realised my own path was never going to be a happy one, if I couldn't be my truest self.

At University I was never interested in getting into a serious relationship. I'd been in one for two years, just before University. After realising we wanted different things, I went off to Sheffield to enjoy the freedom of being young, free and single, like many students do.

The first year I felt free to explore the independence of student life, mixing with new kinds of people from different backgrounds and cultures. I worked hard at my subject and threw myself into all of the new learning on offer. The social side tested my Geordie drinking ability and my personality was being flexed and tested in a new environment. But all in all, I was living an amazing life.

As the second and third years flew by, I regained my own sense of style and individuality, which had occasionally been compromised in the first two years; wearing different clothes, listening to different music and trying new things. My lack of confidence meant I was sometimes trying too hard to fit in, though it was cleverly masked by my confidence in my studies.

I was desperate to prove to people I could choose an Arts degree and still be successful. All of those people that spoke negatively about creative subjects or the Arts, subtly drove me to be great. And in the end, I got what I wanted - a first class degree. I worked all of the hours available around having a part time job, in Tesco's, and partying hard when the weekend came. I made no time at all for relationships.

For a few years of your life and student years, in particular, being in a romantic relationship isn't the top of a lot of people's list. But in your mid to late twenties, it starts to be a different question. When you reach the point of wondering how this life thing is all supposed to unfold, it's easy to hide behind a wall of something else. For me, that wall was being a workaholic.

Sat in my seat, I wondered when I'd be in a position to have a relationship again. It wasn't so much that I wanted a relationship to be happy – it was the way I felt about myself, that was stopping me being able to attract somebody into my life in a romantic or intimate way.

The energy in the seminar space was incredible. Time devoted purely to my individual, spiritual and emotional development. My instinct was that if I was going to reach a place of acceptance and self-love, that's exactly what I needed to do, start to love and accept myself.

I was grateful for the wonderful learning, but for my situation, aggressive techniques of snapping arrows and walking across fire pits; weren't going to be the remedies I needed.

Knowing what was holding me back, was hard to accept and it made my stomach very uneasy. Thinking ahead, I knew I had to be at this place before I'd get to where I wanted to be.

I left feeling excited, re-energised and inspired to continue my journey. I knew what I needed to do.

Chapter 13

# ENOUGH IS ENOUGH

"To be yourself in world that is trying to
make you somebody else is the greatest achievement."

- Ralph Waldo Emerson

Somewhere along the road of life and trying to fit in, trying to be liked and loved, I forgot who I was. In my late adolescent years, a time that there is a lot of pressure to conform and make your own choices, my inner confidence faded. A combination of secondary school, University and entering the uncertainty of the working world, I started to admit how I felt about myself.

Beneath all of the worries of being in a relationship with somebody else, I knew I had to work on the relationship with who I was. My career was going well, and on the surface, my life was probably looking good. I loved doing all the creative work and running educational programmes, all of which I was excelling at because I had a certain level of self-confidence.

However, deep down, I felt a lot of pain. I still felt there was an underlying sense of inadequacy.

I started to think back to where it began, a place that affects most people the most, at school. Even with the best possible parenting and teacher support, school is a place that shapes who you are, the things you choose to do and the image you build of yourself. A little bit of bullying can go a long way to affect people, it was only now I started to realise how badly it affected me.

My primary school was relatively plain sailing, I was well behaved and I worked hard. I had one troublesome spell where I tried to copy the behaviour of the 'cool kids' but thankfully it didn't last very long , I quickly returned to my attentive and hardworking nature.

I was known as little Andy because I was smaller than most people. When I started school, my little feet weren't big enough for black shoes, so I had to wear a pair of blue ones. At age five, small is cute, and as a child, I was oblivious to worrying about my height or blue shoes. However, as you enter high school, where almost everybody is bigger than you, my height was suddenly more of a talking point. Small is no longer cute, small is an opportunity for bullies.

I had a bad start on my first day of secondary school. As a small eleven-year-old in a big comprehensive school, I was daunted by the size of it. I remember walking up a flight of stairs and seeing some much older and bigger lads walking the other way. As I got close to the top, I was lifted up by my neck and carried back down the stairs.

The group of lads all took turns laughing and applauding the boy who humiliated me, my friends could only watch. The only thing

I'd done to deserve it was to be small and light enough to make them look like the strong, cool and clever kids. It wasn't a very good way to start big school.

Another low moment that added to my growing complex about being too small was at football training. When I was fourteen, I went to trials to play for the school team. I played a lot of five-a-side football and played eleven-a-side every week for a club team, but I wanted to see if I could play for the school. I knew it might have been a bit of a challenge, but I was going to give it a shot.

As I walked over to the pitch, I looked down to the field to see it was in good condition and as I looked up, the football manager made his way over to talk to me. Was I going to get some special encouragement? Had he seen me play before? Was he going to inspire me?

No he wasn't. He said very bluntly said, 'I'm sorry to say this but you are too small to play for the team, you won't be able to come to trials'.

I was furious and disheartened, but not confident to stand up for myself. I had to go home.

I thought to myself, how could any teacher say that to a student? Whether I was good enough or not, his decision should have been based on my ability, not on my height. He wanted big, strong, physical lads to build a team that was based on fight. I didn't fit into that picture.

I didn't know what to do. I went home and told my parents what had happened, they were angry and wrote a letter of complaint.

Thankfully they managed to shift my perspective to thinking that if he wasn't intelligent enough to make informed choices and instead make idiotic judgments, I should not waste my time.

I lost my desire to play football for the school team and focused on my club football. Whilst this didn't affect my footballing ability or how much I enjoyed school, it did cement the view I had of myself, of not being big enough, strong enough or man enough to play football. Or perhaps man enough in general. Football meant a lot to people in my local city and my school.

Reflecting on this years later, it was likely I exaggerated this mental link of being too small and let it affect my confidence in other areas of life. It made me care a lot about what other people thought of me.

Until writing this book I probably wouldn't have identified myself as someone who had issues with their body image, but as I look back now and think about how it affected me, I did.

I thought being a man meant being strong and muscular, being tall and handsome. Whilst handsome is subjective, being tall was something I couldn't control, only strong and muscly. For a long time, that's what I thought I was aiming for because that's how I thought I'd be loved.

*

In this new phase of life, living in London, I gradually let those ideas go. I was spending time with people that were open-minded and encouraged me to be forgiving. I met people that had very different views about masculinity and what it meant to be a man. I started to see how important it was that I found love for myself.

As I worked on myself, I started to notice the parts I needed to appreciate more and learn to love; my smile, my stutter and my size, three things that had affected me for years.

From the age of about ten, until my early twenties, I didn't smile for photos. Or at least not a proper smile where I showed my teeth and I looked happy.

For all of the wonderful things I'd done in the previous ten or more years, I didn't smile properly in any photos. Even if I told you I enjoyed it, my face and body said otherwise. Psychologically, I hadn't until this time thought about the affect it was having on me or why I felt so insecure.

I had said to myself 'hide your teeth because they are not perfect..', 'don't smile properly because there is a small gap in between your front two teeth', 'people will judge you and laugh at you'.

The only person that was doing the judging was me. It was a habit that had formed over many years, suddenly it dawned on me as to how significant it could be. If I was afraid of smiling, one of the most natural and beautiful forms of connecting with other people, what else was I hiding? Who was I waiting for to tell me it was okay to smile?

All of these realisations hit me as I stumbled across a little video called 'Validation'. It's a little film about a photographer that likes to make people smile. He meets a young girl who has never smiled and doesn't believe she is beautiful enough to do so. His little quest to make her smile is an inspiring story and one that changed me almost instantly. From that moment forward I gradually smiled more and more, until the point where photo opportunities became a reminder of how far I'd come on my journey.

Thankfully this documentary gave me what I needed. A gentle reminder that I am beautiful just the way I am. Even though I didn't always feel like it.

The other thing I was still conscious of was my stutter. I'd chosen a career than involved a lot of public speaking, so being comfortable with a potential stutter took a lot of work.

I saw a speech therapist when I was really young who said it was very mild and should fade out as I got older. Thankfully, mostly it did. It didn't affect my life as much as stutters and speech impediments can do, but there were times it made me feel unable to do something that most people take for granted.
In my teenage years, I had a phase where I couldn't answer the phone and say a polite "hello?" I'd freeze and be trapped. Eventually, I coped by adding a leading word in front of hello that

somehow made me flow into it. I'd say "erm hello, or um hello" and people didn't really notice. Although, every time I knew the painful feeling was there. I just wanted to say what I was thinking. I'd stumble over my words in a conversation or not be able to say what I wanted, like juddering uncomfortably over speed bumps.

Thankfully, my friends never laughed or judged me for it. For people I didn't know so well, I'd do my best to style it out. I was so embarrassed and ashamed that I was weird or different.

The most significantly challenging time was in English class. I didn't always enjoy English lessons because every time we'd be studying a novel, we'd take turns to read a page out loud. When it came to my turn, I was so petrified of how many times I'd stutter and how people would react and laugh. As I was waiting for my turn, that's all I could think about so I didn't follow the story. It was often the fear of stuttering that was worse than the actual reactions of when I did.

Needless to say secondary school English wasn't as wonderful as it could have been.

Around ten years later, with maturity on my side, I learnt to be more comfortable with the occasional stutter. I cared so much about working in education and doing the work I wanted to do that having a little stutter wasn't going to hold me back.
The final piece of this self-appreciating puzzle I was working through, brought me back to my height. I'd done my best to

forgive the people who made me feel small and I thought I was okay, until somebody set me completely free.

At this point, I am working in the field of training and development. One of the most successful and globally recognised people is Anthony Robbins, a master speaker and life coach. I looked up at him with amazement, in oar of how good he was. He was physically powerful, six foot six and as strong as an ox. Aside from appreciating his talent, I saw him as a stereotypical 'real man'.

Needlessly comparing myself to him, I am five foot seven and quite skinny. I was secretly trying far too hard to emulate other people and not appreciating myself, all until a surprising conversation shifted my perspective completely.

In one of the lunch breaks at the 'Unleash The Power Within' conference, myself and a few friends I'd met there were talking about how amazing Tony Robbins was, his incredible talent and his unrelenting commitment to helping people.

However, one of the girls I was with, was struggling to connect with him. Maybe it was his American accent? Maybe it was the way he delivered his training? No, it was his size. She found that because he was so big, being six-foot-six, it is hard to connect with him on a personal level. She said he was like a giant.

I hope he won't mind me writing this, but I was making judgments about his stature being a great thing. Then I suddenly thought, wow, so it's not always the best thing being really tall, perhaps it was okay I was smaller. All those years I'd grown up believing I was too small, this was an amazing relief. Hearing it from someone else made it really sink in. As much I thought I was content being the height I was, this was a big relief.

Although it was only one other person's opinion, it managed to shatter all of the pre-conceived ideas I had about what it meant to be a man. I left that day so grateful that we had had that brief conversation.

With a little more thinking and a lot more smiling, I started to appreciate who I was and spent a lot less time comparing myself to others. All I wanted was to be authentically me and not feel pressured to be someone else, then I could be happier in life and maybe even find someone to love.

Chapter 14

# THE DARKNESS

"Honesty and transparency make you vulnerable.
Be honest and vulnerable anyway"

- Mother Teresa

2013 was a challenging year. Beneath the guise of being an outgoing, energetic person with lots of energy, I was still carrying a lot of heaviness. I was happier about myself and definitely more confident. There were lots of definite highs, but the lows seemed to get worse.

Living with other people was both a blessing and a challenge. The days I desperately needed company, Kate and James were there. But the days I wanted to be alone and blissfully doing nothing, they were there too. Some days I'd get dressed to create a façade of positivity, other days I'd just keep myself to myself and hope I wouldn't be disturbed.

Being self-employed and freelancing meant my work was intermittent. In the busy times, I coasted on the wave of work and did my best not to think when I didn't need to. But the days and weeks when I didn't have a lot to do were the ones that started to tear me apart.

On my darkest days, it was dreadful. The heaviness of my thoughts and the effort required to do even the smallest things, like get out of bed or make a drink was terrifying. If I could simulate what it felt like I'd get you to put on a suit of heavy armour, give you bags to carry filled with sand and erase every possible positive thought you could have about yourself or your future. I'd stand over you in a patronising fashion and ask you leading questions about the despair of your misery. That's what it felt like being depressed again. Except, I was doing all of this to myself, wrestling with the voices in my head - trying to make them go away.

One conversation kept recurring over and over again. 'I feel alone. Am I ever going to accept who I am? Can I get through this?' I didn't want to force a relationship to happen, but the idea of never finding anyone was scary.

Without researching my medical records in detail, I don't know the exact time I started to slip into a depressive period. But there was a time in 2013 that I was low enough to reach out again for serious support. But this time instead of just going to the GP and asking for more therapy, I went my GP and asked to see a psychiatrist for a diagnosis of bipolar disorder.

My moods were erratic, so unbelievably high and then so crushingly low. I couldn't find a middle ground to live life in a balanced way. I had a lot on my mind and was thinking in circles and circles and more circles. My mind felt like a spirograph, but instead of making beautiful pictures it felt like a jumbled mess. I fell into the trap of using Google again to diagnose myself.

I spoke to my new GP and explained my previous mental health issues. I explained some of the adventures I'd been on and I was clear on what I wanted. I was persuasive enough to convince the doctor to escalate me to see a psychiatrist very quickly. I knew I was depressed and I was relatively okay with dealing with it, but I thought if I have an underlying illness that is causing me further harm, I want to know about it.

I convinced myself that I had severe attention problems, manic episodes and sexuality doubts that were causing extra anxiety and general depression. My housemates were probably aware I was quite down, but they didn't know enough to ask me about it. My parents knew about my depressive times, but I decided I'd keep this one to myself.

A week later I had an appointment to see the psychiatrist. I had mixed feelings of fear, regret, and shame. I decided to walk there to give me some time to think. I was a little anxious about what they might ask me but I was past the point of being afraid of talking about what was going on. I'd felt so much pain that I wanted help.

If you'd have asked me what I was doing there before I spoke to the doctor, my honest answer would have been, 'Deep down I'm really struggling. I'm scared I won't ever be fully happy and I'm scared of the journey I'm on. I want someone to talk to but I don't know who that person is. I want someone as supportive as my mum, but someone that can give me some objective advice. As a bonus, if I could have a diagnosis for a medical illness it would mean I have a disguise to hide behind'.

I knew I shouldn't have really been there. But to convince my doctor that I needed to see a psychiatrist in the first place, I definitely wasn't all sunshine and rainbows inside.

It felt like my last chance. I was going to be truly honest for the first time in a long time.

I sat there expecting to be more nervous. The atmosphere was quite pleasant, a typical room you'd expect from a doctors practice with a comfortable chair in the corner. 'What can you tell me about why you are here?'

'My name is Andy and I'm struggling with anxiety and depression, I think I might have bipolar disorder and there are few other things I want to talk to you about.' I was clear and I got straight to it.

After introducing myself I started to explain my challenges with my mental health. I even had a diagram to illustrate the journey I'd been on, I probably wasn't a typical patient. But then again, I'm not sure there is such a thing. I spoke confidently about how I felt and the level of pain in my low times with a few examples of why I thought I could have bipolar disorder.

I knew I only had one meeting to get some things off my chest. If I wasn't going to be diagnosed with a mental illness, she wouldn't be able to see me again.

The first thing I spoke about was the persistent pain I felt, linked with understanding my sexuality. But after making my point in a slightly embarrassed fashion I skipped on to something else on my agenda.

Out of nowhere, I said – "I think one of my problems is that I masturbate too much." The doctor was a little taken back by my assertion and assured me that it's okay to masturbate and that most men do it.

"Yes I know it's perfectly natural and I have no belief against masturbation or sex. But I know I'm using masturbation to alleviate my pain. It's almost like a drug. I have doubts over my sexuality and I think this behaviour may be contributing to my depression, making me more anxious and giving me the sense of connection I'm probably missing out from in a relationship…and making me feel lonely".

I knew it wasn't good for me and it was so embarrassing to talk about. But after years and years of doing it, I had no idea what it was doing to my brain and my self-esteem, let alone my sex life. I wanted to stop and I wanted to know what it was doing to me.

As for pornography, I think I was introduced to it at about the age of 12 or 13 via some friends as school. The first image I got was hidden inside a word document on a floppy disk. It took so long to load that I lost track of time and my parents came in the room, luckily I managed to pretend it was someone playing a prank. I pulled a shocked face and hid my embarrassment, when I was, in fact, delighted to see some nakedness. From there, it was newspapers and magazines, to late night TV previews, to an online world of everything a young boy/man could ever want. It is frightening to think how things must be now for young people. I could never of imaged how much it could have affected me all these years later.

As I write this I'm sure some people may be shocked about conversations to do with masturbating and pornography. I needed to face this and perhaps other people do too. Or face some other form of compulsive, negative behaviour - this was mine. I needed this conversation to be out in the open.

The problem wasn't masturbation being a part of my life, the problem was when and why I chose to do it.

Anytime I felt overwhelmed or anxious I would turn to masturbation. Sometimes my mind was so active at night, it calmed me down and helped me sleep. It was the easiest way I knew to help release any tension. Sometimes I'd do it to feel in control or to possibly to cement the idea I was straight, or not gay. And sometimes I'd do it for the healthy reason that it feels really good, and every so often is possibly good for you.

Some days the compulsion was so strong I'd feel powerless to not give in, especially when fighting anxiety and depression. Every time I found myself in bed at night or I woke up early in the morning or cocooned under my quilts in a depressive afternoon - I had a way to temporarily lift myself out of the awful dark feelings I felt. I could mask the feeling of loneliness, escape from insomnia and other difficult emotions I was experiencing.

And on top of the habit of excessive masturbation, I usually used pornography to make it more exciting and quicker. To help me get the rush I craved. At the time I'd be lost in a world of lust and pleasure, feeling momentarily free from pain. But that was the problem; it was fleeting and momentary, followed by a tide of guilt and shame.

It was an unlikely place to be having this conversation with a doctor that was assessing me for bipolar disorder.

I wanted to address the cause and I wanted to know the impact it was having on my life. In the previous chapters I spoke about loving myself, this was a whole different meaning of self-love. An act of self-love that was more like self-harm, even if it wasn't life threatening it was gradually damaging my life, my mind, my confidence and my soul.

But this moment wasn't about science, biology or the right and wrong of masturbation. It was about me admitting I had a method to control my anxiety, which I thought was slowly ruining my life. I wanted help. It was against how I believed I should be living my life and I wanted to stop.

On some level I knew masturbating was a natural thing. So rather than putting drugs or harmful chemicals in my body, I knew it wasn't completely bad. I didn't drink a lot of alcohol or compulsively eat to make myself feel good, I masturbated too much and I wanted to stop.

Whilst I wanted to continue the conversation about depression, anxiety, masturbation and pornography, my assessment was coming to an end. The doctor kindly told me I didn't have bipolar disorder and I was okay. She was impressed with how I was able to articulate my journey and be clear on what needed to happen. But she or the service I was entered into couldn't offer me any further support. Unless I had a mental illness, I was in the wrong place.

As I walked home without a mental illness diagnosis, I knew this was something I'd have to work on alone. Maybe this was causing me more damage than I realised. Having the chance to express what I wanted to work on was really valuable, even if it wasn't what the appointment was meant to be.

It was time to go home and reflect on this a bit more.

I wanted to break free from this. Telling the truth about it was definitely a good place to start. Even if it just opened up a deeper search.

Chapter 15
# HIDE AND SEEK

"Expose yourself to your deepest fear,
after that you are free"

- Jim Morrison

That conversation with the doctor set me free from two internal struggles I was having. The first, finding faults with who I was and focusing on what I found difficult, instead of appreciating who I am. Secondly, it gave a voice to something I had suppressed for far too long. It freed me.

In my adventure to diagnose myself as having ADHD, dyslexia or even bipolar disorder, I was desperate to have a label to hide behind. And not because I was undermining the significant challenges people have, that are affected by these conditions, but because I wanted an excuse for my suffering. I wanted a reason to stop living up to my full potential and an excuse to stop me pushing through the discomfort of my current situation.

I made a conscious decision to let go of the destructive behaviour. From here I put a mark in the sand and committed to living a fuller life. One free from blaming my past for my current situation. One free from finding excuses and one free from guilt.

Had I been granted the labels I wanted, it may have given me a short period of relief; it might have made me dance around in my own pity and be smug about the struggles I'd had. But ultimately, if I still wanted to be free from the pain I was experiencing, I had to do something about it. To live at my happiest and live effectively, I'd need to find a way to overcome those things. Deciding to take up yoga was one of the things that radically enhanced my quality of life. It wouldn't be the answer for everyone, but for someone that struggled with anxiety and had a very active mind, the mindful practice that yoga brought me was and is astonishing.

I'd suffered enough from not being able to manage my anxiety. Through my teenage years and at University, and now into my early adulthood. Enough was enough.

It felt good to set free thoughts that were causing me emotional pain. Even though I still wasn't quite free within myself, I'd come a long way. I could almost see the light at the end of the tunnel and I knew what was ahead of me.

The final piece of pain that was still holding me back was the uncertainty I felt about my sexuality. I guess I wanted clarity and some closure after all of the thinking I'd done.

Calling my Mum and telling her I thought I was gay was probably the most painful thing I've ever had to do. I felt so much shame, confusion, anxiety and fear about what it meant for me and my life. But I wasn't afraid of being judged. I knew she'd love me and I knew she'd support me. But telling other people I was questioning my sexuality was horrifying. I felt like telling the first person would be like knocking over a series of dominoes, as soon as I told one person everyone would know.

I was battling with how and if I would tell other people about my sexuality. I was battling with accepting myself. It was holding me back from being happy. It had implications for my life that I couldn't get away from.

I'd spend days depressed in my room, knowing that this was causing me pain. Waking up with a quiet voice murmuring in my ear, telling me to pay attention, telling me to do something to make the pain go away. The familiar dry mouth in the morning, to extreme tiredness despite having fourteen hours sleep. I was tired of being so tired.

I felt like I was playing hide and seek, but nobody was looking for me. There were days I would spend cocooned in my room, hoping someone would come in and pull me out. But no one was coming because nobody really knew.

After another few months of burying the matter, pretending my career pursuits would fill this void, I eventually did something. I took some practical action and attended a Meetup group. For those not familiar with Meetup, it's a platform to organise face-to-face professional or personal 'get together'. The Meetup I was going to was for people that identified as bisexual. I'd never attended one before, but I admired people that started them and acted as catalysts for good conversations and new friendships.

I wanted someone to talk to that understood some of the confusion and anxiety I felt. I didn't know if my struggle was normal. I didn't know how I was supposed to feel. I'd try to mention my doubt to a couple of close friends, but I wasn't confident enough, to be honest about how I felt, because, in truth, I didn't know.

So there I was, embracing a Meetup evening for bisexual people. It sounds very intense when I write it here as if that's the only thing bisexual people are defined by. At the moment I decided to go, secretly signing up, that's all I cared about – how I was labelling myself.

I entered the bar that happened to be in a basement. I expected to feel more nervous but I was fairly relaxed. I was conscious of looking as cool as I could, 'just a normal night, going for a drink, meeting some new people..'.

Thankfully, shortly after I entered a guy called Chris sensed my "I'm new to this group" vibe and my awkward hesitation. I think I said something along the lines of - "I'm quite new to this group, can you tell me what's going on..?" When I really wanted to know; 'what does it mean to be bisexual? How long have you been bisexual? How do you know if you are bisexual? Have you had sex with a man? Do you find men attractive? Do you find women attractive? And most importantly, can you help me be okay with who I am?'

My brain was exhausted - I needed to relax.

After a light introduction to what happened at this particular meet up group, Chris confidently shared a bit about his life. He could probably tell I'd had never met anyone bisexual before, or at least not that I knew about. Without asking too much I gradually got some answers. Simply hearing somebody else express some similar feelings and show complete honesty, especially to someone they had just met was liberating.

After some of the awkward questions were out of the way, we got the chance just to talk as we would meeting anyone new. All of the pressure of acting a certain way and introducing yourself as a particular type of person fell away and normality resumed.

I shared some of my passions and spoke excitedly about the joys of working with young people. Chris shared his passion for acting and reminisced about some of his favourite moments on stage. We exchanged similar experiences of coping with depression and being self-employed, and how we manage the struggle when we are not in work. We both exchanged our feelings of doing work we loved and how lucky we felt. He's asked me if the euphoric highs of doing what I loved, made the unexplainable lows worth it when I wasn't in work? We both agreed they did.

We then got onto the matter of how we both struggled with our mental health, depression and how we stumbled into the bisexual arena - one I was tiptoeing around the edge of like I was ice skating for the first time. Holding onto the handrail at the edge, totally petrified of falling over as the more confident skaters whizzed around.

Like most things, the apprehension of attending this group was totally wasted. Hours and hours, building it up in my mind, painting extravagant worst-case scenario pictures. I was in a room with very "normal" people. And forgive me for ever thinking that being bisexual wasn't a "normal" thing to identify with, as I just didn't have much experience of it. I guess part of the culture and world I grew up in did not always make it seem so acceptable. That's another topic altogether.

At that moment, I was grateful to be in the company of people that I could resonate with. I was happy at the courage I'd shown to take that step and go along. I could have still been imagining terrible things and thinking the worse. I wasn't, I was facing it.

I was with really nice people that happened to have feelings for guys and girls. My inner geek found it all fascinating, even if it was sometimes just enough to distract myself from why I was really there.

As I stood with a beer in hand, pretending it was just a normal party. I started to ask myself some of the questions. 'Do I find these guys attractive? What is right to feel? What is wrong to feel?' All I really wanted to do was chat to one of the cute girls. I sensed it would be harder work than usual as there would be a few extra hurdles in the way.

But I wasn't there to date or try to hook up. I was there to give a voice to a little part of me that had been suppressed for far too long.

I told Chris the story of how I told my Mum I thought I might be gay. I explained the eruption of emotion that poured out of me. How the situation of choosing a house was the catalyst for shaking me up just enough to let it spill out. I told him about how I felt on my lowest days, about how I struggle to get out of bed. How I struggled to see hope in my future and how I struggled to smile when everything felt so confusing.

We had a really nice evening and a couple of drinks. It was probably the most honest conversation I'd ever had, especially in such a short space of time. Honesty, empathy and complete non-judgment, what a space to be in.

I chatted to a few other people more openly than I imaged I'd be able to and enjoyed the rest of the evening.

I was so glad I went along. I exchanged numbers with Chris and hoped to stay in touch.

As I walked back to the tube station, I thought about the pressure I was putting on myself. It was hard to believe how much tension and anxiety that I was letting bubble to the surface. Apart from my Mum, only a couple of other people knew I was struggling with my sexuality. I only told two friends that I had some uncertainty I was dealing with, I didn't think it was okay to be in a phase of questioning. I was so set on being a certain way. Once again trying to define and label myself.

The idea of being gay or bisexual would be another label. For a moment I started to romanticise about the idea of being gay. My ego started to get in the way and reverted to my life being about success and achievements. I thought if I can be openly gay or openly bisexual - I could be confident with myself, I could carry on my journey. I would be able to use my heroic status to make other people happy with their sexuality.

I had to stop myself. I knew I'd been here before. Pretending success and fame would make up for whatever insecurities I felt. I gave that part of me a voice and I needed time to let the dust settle.

As I got home I sat down and tried to forget everything I was thinking about what I "should" do, "should" feel and "should" be and started to be honest with myself. On some level I was able to find guys attractive, but did that make me want to have a relationship with a guy? Probably not at the moment. And I thought about women, 'do I find women beautiful and attractive? Yes, I do.'

Did I need to put this battle to rest? Yes, I did. Would be as easy as that? Probably not.

*

A few days later Chris and I exchanged a few texts saying how nice it was to chat. We arranged to meet up for a coffee the week later. I didn't over think it too much. For once I tried to stop myself thinking and over analysing.

As I arrived at Kings Cross station, a whirlwind of thoughts spun round in my mind. I kept coming back to what was real. The made-up stuff could wait until I went home.

We met in Le Pain, a lovely French café and ordered some drinks. It all happened really quickly. I was doing my best to let my intuition do the talking and enjoy the experience. I was desperately trying to enjoy his company and have a chat, but in the back of my mind was a niggling voice – questioning how I felt and racing into the future.

An hour passed by and we both had to leave for our respective reasons. That was that. I felt mixed emotions; partly a sense of freedom that I was able to do something even if I was partially afraid; and secondly of contentment - I felt good within myself. I didn't have any feelings towards Chris, certainly no lustful or romantic ones. I was there for a chemistry test, to see how my emotional attraction sensor lined up and I left satisfied.

For the first time in many years, I decided I probably didn't need to get trapped into labelling and defining myself. I thought that if I don't know how to describe or identify my sexuality, maybe I didn't need to. Maybe I need to be myself and trust I will meet the right person at the right time. As long as I am happy and loving towards myself, my mind would get out of the way and my spirit would take over. That sounded like a much better plan.

I enjoyed the chat and had a really nice time. I went home with a sense of pride in myself that I'd done something potentially uncomfortable. The Meetup group was a big step into the unknown and to follow it up, instead of retreating again, was an amazing personal achievement.

Whether I was gay or straight, bisexual, neither, or just experiencing a time of questioning my sexuality, I knew I'd let a huge weight off my shoulders. By giving a voice to a part of myself I'd suppressed for so long, I'd created immense freedom in my heart and mind.

I zipped down the escalator, caught a tube to Clapham Common and went home to rest.

Chapter 16

# VALIDATION

*"Loving ourselves through the process of owning
our story is the bravest thing we'll ever do"*

*- Brene Brown*

With a couple of weeks left of the year, I was delighted with how 2013 was finishing. I was getting the hang of being self-employed in London and doing well on the underlying personal development journey I was on. On top of the freelance education work I was doing, I had a few consultancy projects ticking along as well. They fuelled my need for a creative outlet and they topped up my income. So all was looking well.

And it stayed looking that way for the following sixth months too. I got a few nice work contracts that took me to some new parts of England, I took part in a really interesting facilitation course that taught me a lot about experiential learning and for the first time since finishing University, I was earning a decent income.

I allowed the relationship journey to take a little back seat and I enjoyed the beginning of 2014. As a reward to myself for the hard work professionally, I signed up to go a conference in Thailand, one that had been on my radar for a couple of years.

It was time for one more adventure.

Three years earlier in my time after University searching for opportunities, I stumbled across a company called Mindvalley. A very forward thinking and creative company that has a super reputation for employee happiness. Their culture intrigued me and their CEO opened my mind to progressive thinking in the world of business. As one of the world's leading online publishing companies for self-development, it made sense that happiness was at the forefront of the plan. I wanted to learn more.

Once a year they hosted an event called Awesomeness-Fest, an exclusive conference in paradise locations around the world - for entrepreneurs and leaders that want to make the world a better place. For people that want to make a difference and people that put their development at the heart of what they do. I wanted to join.

It really resonated with me so I sent in my application. Back then, sitting in my bedroom in my parent's house, I dreamt of a lifestyle where I get to influence the future of business, dreaming of having an impact on others, dreaming of being in a place to make a great contribution to the world. My application got a response and I had the opportunity to be interviewed via Skype.

I really wanted to go. But deep down I wasn't quite ready. I knew I'd get something out of it and I knew it was my kind of thing, but emotionally I wasn't really in the right place and financially I couldn't have justified it.

Three years later, after earning enough money and feeling much more confident about life, it was time to apply again. Being entrepreneurial and being a leader was something I could say with confidence. I applied and leapt at the opportunity with both feet. I had a Skype interview in March and in June I was on a plane to Thailand!

With my bag packed and a huge smile on my face I was excited beyond belief. I earned this opportunity and I couldn't wait to meet everyone. I was one of two hundred and fifty people from all over the world, we had four days together and I extended the trip to include a holiday too.

In the moments before I set off, I ended up getting a challenge to test my newfound confidence. After all, I was claiming to be an "awesome" person after signing up for a conference called Awesomeness Fest.

On one of the nights, in between the workshops and inspirational speakers, we had a fancy dress party. Fancy dress was one of my favourite things, especially at University. I loved the creativeness of making a costume and I loved the liberating feeling it gave me; to fully express myself and mostly be a little bit silly. It was also a great way to start conversations and break the awkward ice amongst new people - Mindvalley knew what they were doing.

I bought a lovely purple top hat for a cabaret themed evening. As I was deciding whether or not to squeeze it into my rucksack and risk damaging it, James, my housemate challenged me to wear it to the airport.

"If you are going to carry it on the plane, why don't you do something with it?"

"Okay, I like where this is going. What are you thinking?"

"So you are going to Awesomeness Fest....why don't you get a photograph of somebody on the plane, wearing that hat, holding a sign that says 'I am awesome'..?"

Without thinking it through, I accepted the challenge. I left in a hurry and skipped off the airport.

This was an Andy way more confident than the Andy a few years or even months earlier. But still, an Andy that wasn't overly excited by a public challenge. I sat there in the departure lounge - thinking about how this could make a thirteen-hour flight a lot more fun. I carefully tore a page out of my notebook and wrote: "I am awesome".

I suddenly felt extremely nervous about the whole idea. I walked past people with an intriguing smile as if to suggest I was doing something cool but I wanted them to invite me to speak to them. My inner shyness and feeling of not wanting to disturb people meant I walked past about eight possible candidates. This was harder than I thought it would be. I had the sign inside in the hat, with the writing showing in a very uncommitted way.

As I stood at my departure gate waiting to board, I started to rationalise it not being the right place to approach people. "An airport is a serious place, maybe people won't appreciate it...."

Then suddenly I got a tap on the shoulder and a lady said to me "..well, are you awesome?"

She said it with a raised smile but also to challenge me.

"Yes, I am as it happens. I am awesome, so awesome that I'm going to a conference called Awesomeness Fest". I felt quite awkward and didn't want to brag, so I turned to attention to her.

"What about you, are you awesome?"

Her name was Lynn and she is indeed awesome. She was on her way to Australia to babysit for her daughter, a three-day trip and two days of babysitting – I didn't really know what to say other than 'wow'.

She then asked me what I was doing. In a moment of inspiration, I decided to up the anti for my challenge.

"I'm on my way to this conference and I need to get photos with fifty people, wearing this purple top hat and holding a sign that says 'I am awesome". I'm not sure if it was inspired or a silly statement, but before I had the chance to think about it, Lynn grabbed the hat and said she'd be first, followed by her husband. She then gave me a piece of advice that hit me hard.

"I think what you are doing is great, but if you are going to achieve your goal and get fifty people – you need to be more assertive".

I did indeed. I thanked Lynn for the wonderful advice and boarded the plan. I was doing it and I carried on. I chatted to my seat neighbours and they got involved, both sharing their interpretation of what it means to be 'awesome' and some 'awesome' things they'd done. It was wonderful to do something that took the attention away from myself and in turn, allowed me to connect with people in a place I never imagined I could.

I felt really good. Within myself, I did feel awesome. The inadequacies I previously held onto, I'd let go. I was small and proud of my stature. I had an occasional stutter that most people probably didn't even know about. My slim arms were being waved around confidently. My size seven feet were moving with pride. And most importantly, whenever I did something photo worthy I smiled and smiled and smiled.

I stood up to get my own photo taken and pursued my goal, I had a long way to go to get all fifty. I strategically stood by the toilets to get a few people involved, I got the cabin crew and sat back in my seat feeling delighted and inspired. I felt like a journalist writing an article about what it means to be awesome. I had twenty-five photos and I was half way to Thailand.

After a film and some food, I contemplated my satisfaction with getting half way to my goal. "Should I just stop here? Or do I get up and finish this?" Lynn's advice to be more assertive rung in my ears. I was on a plane to a conference claiming to be a leader, I needed to put myself out there. I got back up and carried on with my mission.

As extra motivation, I thought it would make a great entrance story when I meet new people. Instead of boring people with my life story or what I did for a living, I could tell them something cool I did on the plane.

So I did it, with my final surge as we departed the plane, I arrived at the conference feeling full of life and ready for whatever was ahead.

*

At the forefront of my mind was meeting Vishen Lakhiani, the CEO of Mindvalley and the organiser of Awesomeness Fest. Alongside this trip being a reward to myself and another learning opportunity, I couldn't wait to meet him. He'd been a role model in my life for the past couple of years and gave me so much inspiration. It was time to meet my hero.

The location was incredible, a beach hotel in Phuket, Thailand, complete paradise. The staff were kind and welcoming, the atmosphere was calming. I was once again, a long way from what I knew and loving every minute of it. I checked into my room and had a quiet evening to prepare myself for what lay ahead. I'd been on enough courses like this to know that I was in for some intellectual stimulation, but more challengingly, some real emotional soul stirring.

After a pre-event workshop with Lisa Nichols, we were all nicely warmed up for the main event. Being in a space where people were so happy and kind, some , grounded and others bouncing with vibrant energy. I knew I was doing something right to be there. From where my life was just a few years before, I had come an awfully long way.

After the opening ceremony, filled with live music and a warm introduction, I had a chance to meet some of the other delegates and I got my first chance to meet Vishen. I felt a bit like a celebrity groupie, I stood around after he came off stage to say hello. My British modesty allowed other people to have their moment, I stood back, intrigued but anxious. I didn't want to dive into a whole conversation as it didn't feel the right time. I squeezed into the conversation and said a quick hello, frantically garbling my gratitude and I made a swift exit.

The next evening, we were having drinks at the beachside bar. The atmosphere was much more laid back and better to have a good conversation. I really admired the level of success he had reached, the companies he'd built, the positivity and energy of his team and the stylish way he went about his business.

After giving myself a pep talk, I muscled into his conversation. I made eye contact with someone I knew in the group and expected to be welcomed in with open arms. I quickly tried to get the gist of the conversation so I could join in. But whilst the words went in my ears, my mind wouldn't let anything sink in. All I could think about was what I wanted to say. I wanted to tell him stories about the things I'd done. I wanted to impress him and tell him what I was passionate about. I wanted to tell him why I admired his company so much. And I wanted to ask him questions.

I'd built this up a lot in my head. Three years earlier I withdrew my application because I thought I wasn't ready for this event. Now I was stood next to my hero and the inspiration behind a lot of my work. I had so much to say. But as if he read my energy before he read my mind, I must have given off a nervous energy that he didn't like. While I thought I was playing it cool, the desperation creeping out of my manner was enough to turn him away. He didn't want all the fuss and attention; he just wanted to have a drink. He moved away to join another group. The moment had gone.

Luckily, the event had amazing speakers that managed to haul my attention away from my ego and back to why I was there; inspiring me with words of confidence and belief, asking questions that opened my heart and saying exactly what I needed to here at that point time.

The workshop that made the biggest impression on me was by Lisa Nichols, an amazing lady without a homogenous heart and such talent. I met two of her team, CeCe and Margaret, on the first evening. I was drawn to their generosity and kindness. The kind of connections that words can't describe, but deep down you know something special is happening.

Perhaps that's why I was there and that's what I needed most their love and appreciation.

The exercise itself was unlike anything I'd seen before. After setting a tone of compassion and inspiration, we all took part. With our eyes closed, we each took it in turns to walk through a tunnel of people. With their guidance to keep us safe and to move us through, they each whispered words of encouragement, support or inspiration. Words that they would give to themselves and words they'd wish to pass onto other people.

It completely tore me apart. Describing the process will never come near to the emotional expression I felt. I smiled my way through and cried almost every step of the way, and proper tears of joy, releasing feelings that had been hiding away for too long. The voices of eighty people speaking directly to my heart; nurturing me, igniting my spirit and most importantly -reminding me how wonderful and lovely I am.

I didn't expect this. Entrepreneurship and leadership are usually about information and strategies. And personal development was often about bravery and pushing through your limitations. This was nothing like either. And it was everything I needed.

The feelings were equally shared amongst everyone else. We greeted each other with affirming nods, as if to say, that was something special. Especially for me to see other men, fully embracing their emotions and not holding back tears. It was so liberating. The best part was, I didn't feel the need to explain. I just knew that something wonderful was happening in that space. And something wonderful was shifting within me.

Chapter 17

# DREAMLAND

"Respond to every call that excites your spirit"

- Rumi

When I was at University, and I made the decision to go to Summer Camp in America, it was one of the easiest decisions I have ever made. I remember my housemates telling me they were going to get paid for playing sports and being in the sunshine for two months. I loved working with young people and I loved going to new places. I decided on the spot I would go and applied the following day. For some reason, I was so drawn to doing it that I didn't really have a decision to make. It was more a question of how I was going to make it possible.

I was even okay with not knowing where I would be going or what I would really be doing until I got there because it was my kind of thing and it felt right. Somehow, decisions that feel right are a lot easier to make than ones that don't. The decision to come to Awesomeness Fest was a very similar one. The more confident I am, with who I am, and what really excites me, the easier things seem to get.

I loved the experience in Thailand for similar reasons. I loved the trip and I was so glad I decided to go.

The following week I headed to the Phi Phi islands for some welcome relaxation. Being on the other side of the world and in that part of Asia for the first time, it was very tempting to travel and explore. However, I really needed some time to unwind and digest the learning from the conference. This trip was partly a holiday to escape the business of London life and partly a time for reflection. I compromised with myself and decided upon a few days to unwind and a few days to take brief trips to Malaysia and Singapore, where I would fly home from.

Sat on the beach, welcoming the rays from the sun, I held onto a thought that wouldn't seem to go away…

On the final night of Awesomeness Fest, I approached Vishen one last time to have the conversation I wanted to have. Throughout the conference, he showed us some cool pictures of him meeting some of his role models, like Sir Richard Branson, admiring his entrepreneurial prowess and Anousheh Ansari, for her pioneering ambition to explore space. They were people that inspired him, Vishen inspired me and I wanted a photo.

In between a BBQ and a final night of dancing, I smilingly approached him to get a photo together. But to my disappointment, he said he was busy helping his family with something and we'd do it another time. My little heart sunk again and I felt beaten. I just want a photo. Or at least I thought I did.

Sat on the beach in the Phi Phi islands, looking out at the glorious sun, I spoke to my friend Charlotte who I'd met at the conference.

She asked me why it was so important to me. "What was it you really wanted?" I thought about the question for a while.

The question landed in the way I needed it to, leaving me with an inquisitive look and a serious glare. Why was it so important I spoke to him? What did I want him to say that he didn't? How differently would I feel if I did get what I wanted? I pondered it for a while and the answer hit me.

I went all of that way, searching for approval. I wanted him to approve me as someone worthy of success. Despite becoming more confident in myself, I was still waiting for someone else to complete my fulfilment puzzle. Like there was a gap between where I was and my complete happiness, I hoped a few words would pull me to where I wanted to be. In fact, all I did, was keep myself at a safe distance from taking the uncomfortable steps I was afraid of.

I wanted him just to say yes to me perusing my dreams. I wanted him to pat me on the back and say well done for how far I'd come. I wanted him to see himself in me and offer to help me. I wanted his approval.

I still wanted to keep Vishen and his company in mind as a source of inspiration, but I needed to reconnect with myself. I needed the confidence to come from within me. I needed to give myself the permission I was looking for and to do things my way.

Whatever grand plans I had, all of things I wanted to do, I realised that I was the only one who could fully understand. It was up to me to believe in me.

It wasn't until I got home to England that it really sunk in.

*

My trip was coming to an end, home beckoned after a very tiring and emotional trip. I took a short flight to Kuala Lumpur, Malaysia. I went to visit the Mindvalley company office and spent a couple of nights in the city. After reconnecting with some of the other delegates in Malaysia, I took a final trip to Singapore. I went by bus so I could see a little bit of the landscape and gather my last thoughts.

My Singapore trip was a one-night fleeting visit. I spent the afternoon on an open-top bus tour around the city and the evening eating delicious street food. I briefly entered the stunning Marina Bay Sands hotel, that everyone said I had to visit, and went to my hotel. In the morning I squeezed in a quick coffee with a friend called Esther, who I'd met at the conference, before heading to the airport.

We were both in the mood for deep, exploratory conversations about life, continuing one in particular that we started at the conference. Both being in our late twenties, we reminisced about dreams we had as children compared to the dreams we have now. For me, coming to the conference was a dream or a wish I had many years ago, that now came true. It was a magical experience, a luxury private island discussing ideas to make the world a better place, exploring another culture and experiencing the kindness of Thai customs. I was making beautiful friends from all over the world that all made me feel perfect, just the way I am. Esther and I agreed it was a special trip for both of us, a trip that many years earlier we may not have imaged possible.

This conversation sparked an idea well worthy of ending a journey like this.

We both cast our minds back to our earliest dreams and thought about what we wanted to do and be in our lives. My earliest I could remember was wanting to be a cartoonist and work for Disney. When I went to Universal Studios, I was blown away by the process behind the magic cartoons we see in the cinemas. I'm not quite sure I felt it would be a profession or what I'd do with my life, but something about the creative process and the artist flair captured my imagination. I spent hours and hours growing up drawing cartoons, so content in my little word of hand drawn animations. But as school became about grades and achievements, about logical next steps to University and into a stable job, I changed tact to wanting to become an Architect. I chose Maths, Graphics and I.T, I quite liked interesting buildings and I thought it was a job I could be proud of.

As I retold this story, Esther said it sounded familiar and she too chose a career path that was first and foremost acceptable to people around her. I didn't know the first thing about the day to day practice of being an Architect, but it sounded like something society would respect me for.

Esther then said three words that made my eyes light up and my heart sink in the same moment; simultaneously excited by the cleverness and saddened by the feeling it gave me. She said, 'when we are young, it's kind of like we choose 'socially acceptable dreams'. It didn't take long before we both realised those three words abbreviate to S.A.D or sad.

We thought about why we make choices that are heavily influenced by what other people want from us, instead of doing or being who we want to be. We thought about the pressures we have felt throughout our lives so far and the ones we did at that moment.

We tried our best to come up with a more empowering acronym that reflected the opposite, but we didn't quite manage it. Instead, we left the conversation feeling grateful that we'd both managed to step outside of early limiting thoughts about how our life would unfold. That we'd taken chances to spread our wings and explore what the world has to offer. And most importantly, we'd taken the time to get in touch with ourselves, so we truly know what it is that makes us feel alive.

The exciting conversation, almost made me late, I skipped off back to my hotel room to collect my bags. As if the universe was rewarding my new found belief in dreams being possible, I was awarded some final good fortune to round off my trip.

As I departed the hotel, I approached a gentleman that looked like he might also be headed for the airport. He was dressed in general business attire, but not overly smart, I thought I'd ask him if he'd like to share a taxi.

"No thank you, but you can share my limousine if you like? I'm heading to the airport as well..."

"Perfect, that would be great" I said in a very casual and appreciative tone.

So there I was, with my traveller's backpack, full of enthusiasm and zest for life in a Limousine on my way home. I thought it was only polite to make conversation with my chauffeur buddy, though he looked a little pre-occupied with work emails. I told him I'd just been to a conference called Awesomeness-Fest, with a little explanation about socially conscious leaders and entrepreneurs. It turned out he was one of the managing partners of a tobacco and e-cigarette company- needless to say, the conversation didn't start well.

But trying to leave judgement's aside, I found out a little bit about business life in Singapore and how a non-smoker like himself can work in this kind of industry. We pulled into Changi Airport and I thanked him immensely for the glamorous trip. I arrived in style with an extra spring in my step and checked in for my flight. It was time to go home.

After arriving in style to the airport, I was partly expecting my seat to be upgraded to first or business class, instead I got the kind of seat upgrade I never expected.

Before I left for this trip, I was very clear about what I wanted. I wanted to meet fellow change makers, I wanted to develop myself and I wanted to explore the Mindvalley philosophy. I got all of that and a lot of unexpected celebrations too. But on top of that, I was hoping for some time to delve into a meditation or yoga practice. One of the things that has brought the most peace and wellbeing to my life is yoga. Meditation was something I wanted to learn more about and I hoped I'd get the chance to practice it while I was away.

So as if by luck, good fortune or a universal gift, sat next to me on the plane home was a guy who was a practising Buddhist Monk. I found the spiritual teacher I was looking for. For thirteen hours, or as long as he could put up with my questions about the benefits of meditation, I had his company. He gave me his iPod with audio programmes to listen to and told me about his journey to become a Monk; beginning life in England, before swapping it for the sunshine coast of Australia.

I couldn't quite believe what was happening. The way the last days and weeks unfolded were incredible.

I sat back in my seat and enjoyed the last hour of the flight, knowing I'd be back in London before I knew it.

My journey was almost complete and just beginning.

Chapter 18

# BEING A HERO

"The only thing that you have that nobody else has is you.
Your voice, your mind, your story, your vision.
So write and draw and build and
play and dance and live as only you can"

- Neil Gaiman

I was back in a familiar reality. In my small bedroom, in a shared flat on Wandsworth Road, in a city that people are racing around – welcome back to London. The tropical beaches of Thailand and the fresh coconut water seemed so far away.

I waited patiently and excitedly for James and Kate to come home from work, I couldn't wait to catch up. I was conscious that not everyone would understand my trip to Awesomeness Fest, even the name is probably strange enough. Thankfully James and Kate were open minded and embraced my weirdness, enthusiasm and adventurous spirit.

As soon as they got home I greeted them with gifts. I shared the success of my 'I am Awesome' project with my housemate James, who instigated it in the first place, he was proud and inspired! On his next holiday he followed suit with a challenge in New York, getting a whole train carriage of New Yorkers to send Kate and I a message.

I told Kate about some of the things we did, knowing she'd be interested and certainly approve of the exotic locations we got to visit.

Thankfully, enough of my friends wanted to hear about the magic that happened and were starting to see changes in me - the gleaming smile on my face, the openness in my heart and the extra freedom to be myself.

*

I stopped to breathe and called my family to relay my general delight with life.

I spoke to Mum first to thank her again for the support she'd given me over the past few years. I didn't expect mum to understand how I felt, but I hoped she sensed how far I'd come and I hoped she was proud of me. I hoped she'd feel a little bit more relaxed that my life was well under control. From where I was in March 2011, to just three years on in September 2014, I'd come a long way.

While speaking to Mum on the phone, it dawned on me what had happened. While a did my best to listen to my Mum's stories about her choir practice and interesting goings on at work, I felt my eyes bubble with emotion. I didn't say anything, but I felt overwhelmed inside.

I started to realise the journey I'd been on and I realised who made it all possible; the great talks, the inspiring people, the experiences I've had, only a few of which I've described here. I felt so lucky. But most importantly, I'd been all the way to Thailand to meet my hero, to get back and realise that my biggest hero was with me all along.

My real hero is my Mum.

I'm emotional writing this and I know my Mum will be reading it too. It's really difficult to put into words and convey my gratitude. The love, support, patience and kindness. The belief, listening, guidance and faith. The stuff words can't even describe, but deep down we know what it's all about.

Without my Mum, this elaborate and often arduous journey of self-discovery wouldn't have been possible. Or at least it would have taken me a lot longer and I'd have suffered way more than I needed to. Since I first crashed to my knees, from the big moments to the smaller ones, I've known she was there for me – whenever I needed her.

As soon as I got off the phone, I let a few tears of emotion run down my face. I continued my thought train of gratitude to all of the people that have helped me on my way. My Dad and my family, my Auntie and Uncle, James and Kate, Terence and my other friends of which I am so grateful. And to all of the spiritual teachers that guided me in their presence and through their work, to so many people I have immense gratitude.

They gave me the space to learn and the courage to keep going when I wanted to give up. They inspired me to let my true passions shine. They inspired me to try new things and be brave with my life. They taught me to be grateful and kind as often as I could. Most importantly, they taught me to find within myself a level of acceptance and peace that made me feel alive and live an awesome life ahead.

To look back now and consider my initial episode of depression not happening, is almost worse that remembering the painful feelings of being there. I know I would never be as happy and content as I am today without going through it. I wouldn't have been forced to show humbling vulnerability, I wouldn't have seen how generous and loving people can be. I'd never have connected with people on such a real and personal level. I'd never have uncovered some of the personal insecurities that were holding me back and never have taken some of the opportunities in recent years that have brought me such joy. And I wouldn't have gained the empathy to relate to other people that are suffering in their own way.

I actually learnt what it means to be someone's hero.

Before I went through my first phase of being depressed, I honestly had no idea what it really meant. I didn't know how dark or helpless I'd feel and I definitely couldn't have imaged there was anything to learn by going through it. In my lowest moments, it was hard to feel anything good. And in those moments I didn't understand how it would get better. I guess a little part of me knew that if I believed enough and did what I needed to do, it would be possible to recover.

I look forward to my life knowing it's going to be okay, and at times it will be great and I'm way more prepared for the next chapter, whatever it may bring. It taught me to trust and have faith in something outside of myself, to let my heart lead the way, to be honest as much as I can, to appreciate myself and the life I have, to take the initiative to make things happen and most of all to live life with enthusiasm.

From that moment, sitting in my little room, with tears rolling down my cheeks, a smile on face and a whirlwind of creative energy fizzing in my mind, I knew I had a story to tell.

It felt like the end of a long journey and the beginning of a new one. I was bursting with inspiration, new things I wanted to do, more confidence to express myself and happier than I'd ever been before.

I decided to tell this story that felt trapped inside me. I didn't know how or when I'd have the courage or the ability to express it, but I knew I had learnt so much I wanted to help other people that were navigating a similar journey. People who wanted to move from existing in their life to truly living, people who were making important decisions and wanted to connect with the truth of their heart. People who have struggled with their mental health and wellbeing or know someone that is and to support people who want to embrace the full potential of who they really are.

After feeling very lost and losing my way, both on my career path and within myself, I found what I need to and I did it. From this moment forwards, I've got to keep living and keep navigating this beautiful journey of life. The same I wish for you.

Whatever living on purpose means for you, whatever you are working towards in your life; let it be a journey of discovery, hope and courage.

Wherever you are, I trust that you will find your way.

Much love,

*Andy*

# An Invitation

# Ten Things I Learnt

I'm conscious that a lot of what I wanted and needed to say, I've said and I'm aware that my decision to share this story is possibly more important in itself, than the words I chose to share. So with that in mind, I hope this has been a valuable read, I hope it has made an impression on you and I hope I get to meet you, to say thank you for reading it.

Before I do say my last words, I have one final invitation, to spend some time reflecting.

Whilst this story alone may reach people in the way they need, it may have sparked some questions and given some people answers, my early readers requested some more practical guidance.

I spent some time digesting the learning that I have personally experienced, in the hope it helps you reflect in your own way. I expect each of you will take different things depending on when you read this and what's going on in life at the time.

I have been helped immensely in my journey and this book is one of the ways I want to pay my gratitude forward to others.

1.

Listen to your heart,

it's there to guide you for a reason.

At the beginning of this story, I had a choice to make as to whether or not to pursue a certain career path and relocate cities. Instead of listening to my intuition, I ignored it and searched for something else instead. I chose to reject it for as long as I could until the anxiety got too much - the panic attacks were a very loud wake-up call.

I learnt that sometimes, seeds of doubt are not fears, they are indicators that we aren't walking down a path that is right for us. Sometimes we need to think things through and be logical, and other times we need to trust our instincts. The thing to know and practice; is when to think with our heads and when to listen to our hearts.

What is your heart telling you?

2.

It's okay not to be okay,
it's courageous to ask for support.

When I first admitted I was struggling, I didn't know what was going to happen. When I called the Samaritans and when I turned up at the doctors for a diagnosis of depression, I was very confused. Those moments were turning points for me acknowledging I needed help.

I learnt that it is okay to ask for help and it's a brave thing to do. Before this journey, I thought being brave meant holding in my struggles and not telling people how I was feeling. I know now, the opposite is true. When we are able to show our true feelings and ask for help when we need it, we show true courage.

What courageous step could you take?

3.

Honesty connects us,
being real is a gift to others.

Crying in front of my Mum for the first time as an adult, was one of the hardest things I've ever done. In a moment when I was most vulnerable, my Mum opened her heart and showed a level of compassion I'd never seen before. From that moment on, I thought about honesty in a very different way. I was encouraged to be more honest with friends, family and colleagues about other things too.

I learnt that honesty can be freeing for us, allowing us to be ourselves and it can also give others the opportunity to open their hearts too. If we don't open up and be truthful, we can't expect others to either. If we do open up and show the real us, we allow others to do the same.

What do you need to be honest about?

4.

Be grateful for what you have,

appreciate where you are.

When I decided I wanted something else from life, I quickly learnt to dislike my part- time job in Tesco's and became frustrated living with my parents. I thought I deserved something more and I started to think about where else I could be. Whilst feelings of anger, disappointment and frustration can be the catalysts we need to change something in our lives, they won't move us forward and they won't make us happy.

I learnt that it's okay to want things to change and it's very natural to want your life to progress, but being appreciative on the journey, is the only way we can truly be happy. Wherever we are, we can always find something to be grateful for.

What could you be grateful for?

5.

Life is yours to create,
it's up to you to make it happen.

Jetting off to San Francisco, entering a design competition and moving to London to start youth work, were all moments I was proactive. Even not knowing exactly what I wanted, I took the initiative and made things happen. Looking back over the last few years of my life, many of the successes I've had, came from saying yes to opportunities.

I've learnt that sometimes we need to be patient and other times we need to take a leap of faith. It may not always work out straight away, but it may lead us to the next place we need to be. The more we get out there, the more opportunities seem to come our way. It's up to us to create the life we want.

What will your next leap of faith be?

6.

Know yourself,
decide what's important to you.

As I progressed with my freelance lifestyle, the ability to be creative, the freedom to follow multiple interests and the desire to make a difference through my work, all appeared as things that were important to me. The more I got to know myself, my values and my interests, the easier it was to make decisions about what to do.

I learnt the importance of reflecting on my values and current priorities in order to find the best way to feel fulfilled in life. The more uncertain we are, the easier it is for other people to influence our thinking. When we know what's important and we make choices in line with those desires, we have a way to be really happy.

What is important to you?

# 7.

Suffering can set us free,
hard times don't have to define us.

Admitting I was struggling with my sexuality, discovering how insecure I was about my body and acknowledging my behaviour with pornography, were all things causing me immense heartache. The darkest times and struggles with depression, forced me to look within myself and get to the root cause of my pain.

I learnt that low moments in our lives can be the ones we need to make us push through to another level of living. The confidence I have, the way I smile with joy and the freedom I feel to be myself, were all thanks to hard times. Suffering could be an opportunity to really break free.

What would set you free?

8.

Be open and try things,
don't let fear and judgment stop you.

Doing improvisation theatre classes for the first time and going back to yoga after pushing through some mental hurdles, were both life-changing decisions. Yoga became a weekly ritual that I still love and couldn't imagine being without, and improv theatre lead me to build a career around creative facilitation and training.

I learnt that sometimes we need to trust other people's advice, especially when they know us really well. Whilst fear may always be a factor in our lives, we can learn to not let other people's opinions stop us doing things we want to do. When we try things with an open mind, we expand our comfort zones and we learn to live life in a very exciting way.

What will you commit to trying?

# 9.

Trust your journey,
have faith in the bigger picture.

When I went to India at eighteen years old and did a course in personal development, I had no idea that ten years later I'd be working in education or writing a book to help others. When I left university, I didn't know how I'd apply my creative skills or how saying yes and no to certain opportunities could possibly work in my favour.

I've learnt that if we follow a path that feels true for us, over time we'll be able to see how it all fits together. I've learnt to trust that everything will work out as it's meant to, especially if we see it that way. We just need to let go of control, surrender enough and allow what's meant to be.

What do you get the most joy doing?

# 10.

Love who you are,
being yourself is the greatest gift of all.

I'd never really questioned the possibility I was ever being insincere, but looking back I was afraid so of being judged, trying desperately to fit in and meeting other people's expectations. Without confidence and positive self-esteem, we chase other things to make us feel good and we project our own internal pain onto people.

I've learnt that the more comfortable we are with who we are, the less time we spend comparing ourselves to others. The more we can appreciate our own beauty, our own talents and accept the things that make us who we are, the easier it is to live the life we want to lead.

What makes you who you are?

# My Final Thoughts

It's now 2016, the Summer is almost over and the leaves are beginning to fall. I've just finished doing yoga at my usual Tuesday night class. After practising for a few years, I feel confident that I know what I'm doing (I know enough to look like I do anyway).

In the middle of a deep back bending posture, I see this journey for what it really is; the hour-long yoga class, my life so far and the years to come. It's not a place for comparison, judgment or being the best, though it's an easy trap to slip into, it's a place for showing up and giving it the best you can.

It's admittedly terrifying to publish a book about "life stuff" at what could be considered a young age. However, the expertise I am claiming is that I know myself way better than I once did. I have had an immensely valuable learning journey and I'm fortunate enough to have a gift for communicating and inspiring others — so I must continue to so, to be in alignment with my happiest self.

When I wrote the title of the book, I was about three chapters into my first draft. At that point, the title of the book emerged to be 'Living on Purpose'. Right until the month before publishing, that was the title.

On this journey over the last few years, through living more freely and writing out this story, I discovered the idea of living on purpose. I want it to be an invitation for people to live their life in their own inspired way. A way of guiding the choices we make, to encourage us to express ourselves in an honest, happy, confident and free way; to take opportunities that align with our hearts and spirits; to make the most of life, to make plans that excite us and create the life we truly want to live.

Importantly, it is also an invitation to express the emotional side of ourselves when things are hard; making it okay to acknowledge times we struggle and feel down, as long as we take steps to overcome the source of our pain.

At this point, living on purpose is an extension of the story in this book. It's a reminder to myself, to make decisions with the best interests of myself or others at heart. It's not always easy but that's what I strive to do.

This identity has empowered me over the last few years to ensure I am, with my own definition, living on purpose.

The same I invite you to do.

However you decide you want to live life, you can measure your own sense of fulfillment and prompt yourself to make changes when you need to. You can evaluate the different areas of your life to see where happiness lies and where change needs to occur. You can make choices every single day to create the life you want, to overcome challenges, to heal your spirit and to live vibrantly like the wonderful human being you truly are.

With so much love, embrace your journey.

# Writing This Book

I hope this book serves as a gift to many people, but first and foremost, the writing process alone was a gift for myself.

It's been a process that's been so cathartic and freeing that journaling and diary writing has become a part of my life, almost on a daily basis. This extra weight of being ready to write what I felt, as well as being disciplined to sit down and do it was different to anything I've experienced before. I've said to many people, that even if I didn't publish it, I'm so much better off by committing to this process. One of my favourite quotes is by Brene Brown "Owning our story is the most powerful thing we'll ever do."

For over two years I worked hard to get this story out onto paper. It's been quite something to put this into words and it's opened me up in ways I didn't expect. It forced me to clarify the wavering memories in my mind and give the uncomfortable stories a useful meaning.

After five versions and several edits, printing numerous paper copies and cutting it to pieces to re-order the story, I have a book I'm proud of sharing with you - something perfectionism and fear could have stopped me from finishing and sharing.

I hope this story inspires you to express parts of your own story in a way that feels right for you.

# Support for Mental Health and Emotional Wellbeing

For many people, this book may have brought up some challenging thoughts and feelings, particularly regarding mental health. If you feel that seeking support would be the right thing to do, even if it feels like a daunting step, please reach and do so. It takes immense courage to do so. Asking for help is a brave and positive step.

It may be speaking to a trusted friend or family member, a teacher or a member of staff, a colleague or dedicated support person, or may be seeking professional support.

These organisations give all kinds of help, such as advice, counseling and emotional support.

Sometimes one conversation can make a big difference.

1. NHS Direct

Non-Emergency medical advice from trained health professionals on all issues connected with physical and mental health.
Contact 111 (in the UK).

2. Your local GP

Your local GP can prescribe treatments and therapy programmes. They can refer you to specialists for longer term help.

3. The Samaritans
www.samaritains.org

Confidential emotional support for people experiencing feelings of distress or despair. Open 24 hours, 7 days a week.
Call: 116 123 (free phone)

4. Young Minds
www.youngminds.org.uk

Information about mental health and emotional wellbeing.

5. CALM
www.thecalmzone.net

Support for men, specifically to prevent male suicide.

# Books I Recommend

Here are a few books that helped me get to where I am today. Some are more practical and others are more spiritual. Enjoy when and if, they feel right for you.

- 7 Habits of Highly Effective People by Steven R. Covey
- Daring Greatly by Brene Brown
- A Return to Love by Marianne Williamson
- The Power of Habit by Charles Duhigg
- Breaking the Habit of Being Yourself by Dr.Jose Dispenza
- Zero Limits by Joe Vitale
- The Alchemist by Paulo Cohelo
- Unlimited Power by Anthony Robbins
- Yoga and the Path of the Urban Mystic by Darren Main
- The Leader Who Had No Title by Robin Sharma
- The Highly Sensitive Person by Elaine N. Aron
- 100 Days Happier by Domonique Bertolucci

I'll share other useful videos and resources online at www.andydunn.co

ANDY DUNN